THE JEWELRY ARCHITECT

KATE McKINNON

techniques + projects for mixed-media jewelry

Editor: Jean Campbell
Art Director: Liz Quan
Designer: Lee Calderon
Photo Stylist: Ann Swanson
Production: Katherine Jackson
Photography: Joe Hancock
Step Photography: Joe Coca

Interweave Press LLC
201 East Fourth Street
Loveland, CO 80537-5655
interweave.com

Printed in China by Asia Pacific Offset Ltd.

Library of Congress Cataloging-in-Publication Data

McKinnon, Kate.
 The jewelry architect : techniques and projects for mixed-media jewelry
/ Kate McKinnon.
      p. cm.
 Includes bibliographical references and index.
 ISBN 978-1-59668-176-7 (pbk.)
 1. Jewelry making. I. Title.
 TT212.M39254 2010
 739.27–dc22
                         2010012421

10 9 8 7 6 5 4 3 2 1

ACKNOWLEDGMENTS

I have always wanted to be the kind of artist who takes the time to talk to eager beginners about their work, and who freely answers questions about technique or craftsmanship. I love people like that. I carry the generosity of people who took this time with me, particularly Allison Shock, Pamela Engebretson, Gail Crosman Moore, Dustin Tabor, and Kate-Drew Wilkinson.

Special thanks go to my friend Scott Bartky, whose gentle spirit and open intelligence helped me make sense of my own obligation to always keep an eye out for an opportunity to do my work more simply, elegantly, and cleanly. Scott lived by the idea that one can have a caper-filled, exciting existence, be a precise craftsperson, an eager student of life, a responsible scientist, and also run your life and studio in a way that also helps others. I miss you, Scott, and am grateful for the chances I had to work with you.

CONTENTS

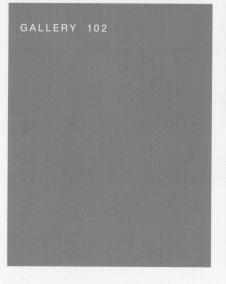

INTRODUCTION

One of our most charming human traits is our love of ornament and architecture. Since the days of the cave, we've been picking up shells and stones with holes, using plant and animal fibers for stringing material, and digging treasure out of the ground to ornament our bodies and dwellings. Most other animals content themselves with nature as they find it; not us. We want to paint it, bejewel it, rearrange it, and sparkle it up. Some of the ornament we make seems to spring from our very souls, and be about our need for mythology, religion, or symbolism. Some springs from our desire to leave behind something of beauty, something that will survive us and continue to give joy or to impress the world with our magnificence, our generosity, or our wealth long after we are gone. Me, I just like to see how elements combine; I like colors, transition areas, connections, and joins.

I am inspired by clever solutions, by clean connections, and by those who explore not only the edges of their creativity, but the limits of their materials. I am always looking for a better way to do things, and like an octopus, or a bower bird, two creatures that do share our love of bits and bobs, I am constantly surrounded by small treasures and found objects that cry out to be set, hung, pierced, bezeled, or otherwise made wearable.

I find artists on the whole to be a very curious bunch, and almost everyone I know who makes art works in several media. Jewelry seems to fill my creative urge in a variety of ways. I love the smallness of it; it's manageable and can be made in almost any type of space. I can incorporate painting or photography, and I love the combination of precise and free thinking that goes into making small works. So far, I'm content to work in miniature.

The projects in the book use a wide variety of materials, including beads, metal, and wire, and showcase a variety of ways to make settings or to string, hang, or present your favorite ornaments. Whether we are working with beads, wire, metal, or felt, you can see the overlap in components, design, and the principles of connection. Each way of making jewelry presents its own strengths and weaknesses, and I use them all, drawing on what works best for the specific needs of each piece.

When making a piece, my focus is on how to bring what I know about movement, connection, longevity, and presentation to its design, and to further those aims, I work in any material and use any technique that can help me.

If there are techniques shown here that you haven't tried yourself, or materials you haven't yet played with, I encourage you to experiment and perhaps add something new to your own repertoire as a designer.

Recycled Bottle beads by Bronwen Heilman.

ELEMENTS

I consider myself primarily a maker of components, an engineer of connections. I spend most of my creative time making bits and pieces, elements and sections and clasps, and only when the mood strikes do I assemble them into finished pieces. Working this way gives me great freedom as a designer, as there is little pressure to produce specific results, especially those based on a fixed idea that I or someone else had. When I sketch, or when I daydream about making things, I am usually focused on things such as areas of joinery or small ideas for engineering that grow into bigger ideas for finished pieces. My finished jewelry is usually an illustration of some concept I had about movement, structure, or an improvement on a common theme. Presented in this section are some of my favorite essential components, each of which is open to almost limitless variety and interpretation.

CLASPS

1.1 SCULPTURAL S-HOOK
1.2 REMOVABLE BALL-END CLASP
1.3 SIMPLE TOGGLE CLASP

EAR WIRES

2.1 SIMPLE EAR WIRES
2.2 SCULPTURAL
    ONE-PIECE EARRINGS

RING FINDINGS

3.1 RIVET POST RING
3.2 WRAP RING

Lampworked beads by Joyce Rooks.

CLASPS | 1.0

I began making clasps because I wanted better options for closing my sewn work. I dislike sewing beadwork directly to connecting elements, and I wanted components that were designed to flow with the delicate fabrics of my weaves. In this section I'll show you several of my favorite closures: a fine silver wire Sculptural S-Hook, unusual for its ornament of hand-formed fine silver metal clay at the tip, and ideal for fastening handmade chain; a nifty (and removable) Ball-End Clasp for sewn beadwork; and a simple toggle-ring closure, perfect for including in beadwork, strung jewelry, or chain mail.

1.1 | SCULPTURAL S-HOOK

MATERIALS

- 3" (7.6 cm) of 12-gauge or 2" (5.1 cm) of 14-gauge fine silver wire
- ½ g or less of fine silver metal clay

TOOLS

- Large round-nose pliers, ring mandrel, or multi-sized Wrap and Tap tools
- Flush cutters capable of cutting 12-gauge wire
- Chasing hammer
- Anvil or steel block
- Tumbler (optional)
- Buffer (optional)
- Burnisher (optional)
- Patina solution (optional)

This beautifully designed hook is crafted with a sculptural metal clay tip fired onto a length of drawn wire. Pieces like this are one of the most useful applications for metal clay at a traditional jeweler's bench, because you can take advantage of the natural density and strength of wire as well as enjoy the sculptural expression of metal clay. Working this way offers the luxury of having a finished piece in your hand with only a few minutes of work at the bench. Carving a wax model and casting is the only other way to sculpt a tip and is not only time-consuming but requires specialized equipment.

1 Roll a 2–4 mm ball of metal clay, texturing it if desired, and spear it on one end of the wire to form a small sculptural tip on one end. I usually choose to roll my ball smooth, spear it, and then press the speared ball and wire compressively against a texture sheet, to form a triangular tip, but anything that pleases you will work as a tip as long as the embed is clean and snug. Allow the metal clay tip to thoroughly dry.

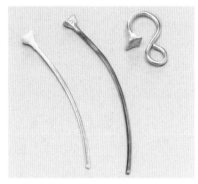

Sculptural S-hooks in various stages: cut wire with drying clay tip; the fired and patinated ornamented wire before bending; and a finished, formed hook.

2 Carefully inspect the metal clay tip to make sure it doesn't fall off of the wire when you turn it upside down. If it does, you didn't make a snug enough embed. If necessary, remove the tip and fill the hole in the metal clay with syringe clay or a small ball of freshly rolled metal clay. Re-embed the wire into the filled hole, let it dry again completely, and you should find that it's now nicely stuck on. Don't attempt to fill gaps around an embed with slip; it's not dense enough to use as a glue and will form a weak bond. You want the tip so sturdy you can forge it if you like, and no slip bond can withstand forging.

3 Fire the wire for at least one hour at 1,650°F (899°C) if possible. If you're using a wire that can't take that much heat for that long, such as sterling silver, drop the temperature according to what your metal of choice can stand. I only use fine silver wire for this job because I want to fire everything I make in metal clay for two hours at 1,650°F (899°C). If I fire this long, I know that the resulting pieces can stand up to forming, sizing, and forging. If you compromise on your firing time or temperature, you must also compromise on how far your piece can go at the metalsmithing bench.

4 After firing, and before you do any finishing work such as tumbling or forging, manually turn the dead-soft wire around a round form, so that it makes a beautiful S shape. To do this job, I use large round-nose pliers for the small loop of the S. To form the larger loops, I use either the 10 mm section of a small Wrap and Tap tool for a 14-gauge hook or the 13 mm or 16 mm segment of a large Wrap and Tap tool for a 12-gauge hook. Those are the sizes I use most often, but you should form your hook to the shape and size that suits your design or the chain you're hooking into.

   It's easiest to use Wrap and Tap tools to form the hooks because they hold the wire firmly while you form it, and the soft vinyl sheath on the holding jaw will not mar the surface of the wire. You can use dowels or mandrels, of course, but you'll have to hold the wire down with your fingers while you turn it. Not everyone is comfortable doing this with 12-gauge wire.

5 Forge the hook, if you like, by hammering the wire section flat on an anvil or block. You'll have best results if you use a smooth chasing hammer with rounded edges, and you use your hammer to stroke, rather than to compress the metal. Forge the hook from both sides, attempting to be very even with your metalwork. If you hammer on one side, ideally you should hammer on the other as well. Keep in mind the matrix of individual metal grains; you want the stresses to be as even as possible, and the finished piece to be nicely compressed, smooth, and strong.

6 Buff, burnish, patina, polish, or tumble the formed hook to taste.

7　Attach the hook to your chain or finished piece by using flat-nose pliers to gently open the small end of the S. Connect the chain and close the hook. Lightly hammer the closed section of the hook on the edge of an anvil or block to work-harden it in its final form.

Note: Don't attempt to open and close the finished hook more than a couple of times. If you do, you'll stress the metal. If you need to bend it more than three times, anneal the hook by warming it to a pink glow with a torch or in the kiln. Allow it to cool and then re-forge it to work-harden it for duty again. If you anneal the hook, you'll need to reapply any patina, as the heat will burn off any color that you added.

Note: The Sculptural One-Piece Earrings (page 17) and Cocktail Pod Ring (page 92) are built in the same way as this hook, with sculptural ornaments added to the tip of forged wire. ■

1.2 REMOVABLE BALL-END CLASP

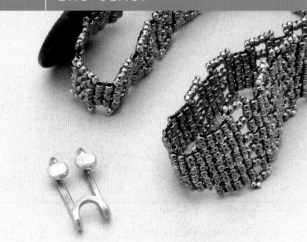

MATERIALS
- 5"–7" (12.7–17.8 cm) of 12- or 10-gauge fine silver wire
- ½ g or less of fine silver metal clay

TOOLS
- Sturdy flat-nose pliers
- Chasing hammer
- Anvil or steel block
- Tumbler (optional)
- Buffer (optional)
- Burnisher (optional)
- Patina solution (optional)

This innovative and simple clasp will slip easily in and out of beadwork cuffs to which you have added tubes or sleeves at each end. You can bend a custom clasp to any width that suits your piece, and I could imagine it as a closure for fabric and felt work, as well as beadwork. The clasp was inspired by the way that quilts are hung; a secondary channel is sewn along the back of the quilt, so that the bar used to hang it on the wall does not stress the handwork of the body of the quilt.

1　You can use any wire for this clasp, as long as it can take the heat of the firing cycle to fuse the balls or sculptural tips to the wire. Fine silver metal clay can be fired as low as 900°F (482°C), although you will always

have best results at 1,650°F (899°C) for two hours. If you do choose to underfire or short fire your ball ends, be sure not to cheat on time; give them at least an hour in the kiln to bond to the wire. Explore various sculptural shapes and textures at the tip of these clasps for variety.

Grasp the wire in the middle with sturdy flat-nose pliers. Use your fingers to bend the wire up on both ends to form a flat-bottomed U shape. Ideally, the two legs of the U will be exactly even; if they aren't, trim the longer one so it's even with the shorter one. If you are making this clasp to fit a specific piece, measure the sleeve the ball end will fit and be sure that after turning the wire into a U shape, there is enough leg to go through the sleeve, with an extra ¼" (6 mm) on each end. The ball ends will be speared on the ends of these legs, and the balls will be turned down after firing.

2 Use the chasing hammer and anvil or steel block to forge the U-shaped wire to taste, using stroking blows and holding the legs together. As you do so, they won't spread open as you hammer. Remember to forge smoothly, from both sides.

3 Roll two 4–6 mm balls of metal clay and spear them on the ends of the wire (see Rolling Metal Clay, page 128, for help with this job). The success of your clasp will depend on clean, snug embeds, so don't manipulate the balls once they are speared. If you feel the embeds aren't tight enough, remove the ball, quickly reroll it so it doesn't dry and crack, and re-spear it on the wire.

4 Allow the metal clay ball ends to dry completely. Turn the clasp upside down to see if the balls fall off. If they do, fill the holes in the balls with syringe clay or tiny balls of fresh clay, re-embed the U wire, and allow to redry. Test again before firing.

5 Fire for two hours at 1,650°F (899°C).
   If you're using wire than can't take the heat of this firing, drop your firing temperature accordingly. If you short-fire or underfire your metal clay, though, you will not be able to forge or form the balls after firing.

6 Clean and polish the clasp as is, or you may wish to use flat-nose pliers to grasp the balls and turn them at a 90° angle to the body of the U so that they have a better grip on your beadwork. This may or may not be necessary, depending on the size of the ball ends and the design of your beadwork. I normally make these clasps about ten at a time, in different sizes, and choose to turn or not turn them when I am selecting them for a finished piece of beadwork.

7 Once you are satisfied with the shape and form of the clasp, buff, burnish, polish, and patina to taste. ■

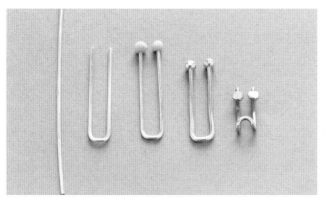

Ball-end clasps in the different stages of forming, *left to right*: the straight, cut wire; the speared fresh clay ends; the fired clasp; and one that has been bent both top and bottom to fit a very small piece of beadwork.

1.3   SIMPLE TOGGLE CLASP

MATERIALS

- 1" (2.5 cm) of fine silver 18- or 16-gauge wire
- 1 fine silver 6mm closed ring
- 10 g or more of fine silver metal clay

TOOLS

- Flush cutters
- Round-nose pliers
- Metal clay work surface, roller, texture sheet(s), and circle cutters or X-acto blade
- Kiln
- Chasing hammer
- Anvil or steel block
- Buffer (optional)
- Burnisher (optional)
- Tumbler (optional)
- Patina solution (optional)

This clasp is done with a combination of metal clay and fine silver wire. If you prefer a bit of chain on your bar instead of a single ring, the most efficient way to include it is to make the chain first (see Fusing Fine Silver, page 137) and capture it on the U bail before embedding. Rings and chain can certainly be fused or soldered onto the U bail after the bar is complete, but it's more time-consuming to do it that way. Experiment with different shapes of ring and inner opening and with different styles of bar.

1. Use round-nose pliers to bend the wire into a small U shape, about ⅛" (3 mm) wide and ¼" (6 mm) long, with nice straight legs. Remember to leave enough leg to not only embed into your fresh clay bar, but to remain above the surface for use. Trim the excess wire and set the finished U bail aside.

2. Roll and texture a sheet of fine silver metal clay to a finished thickness of four to eight cards. (See Rolling Metal Clay, page 128) Cut a circle out of the textured sheet that suits your piece; my standard size for the exterior is about 1¼" (3.2 cm) in diameter. Out of that circle, cut another smaller circle for the bar to pass through, about ½" (1.3 cm) in diameter. Make this inner circle about ⅛" (3 mm) from one edge. Don't cut closer to the edge or you may damage the structure of the toggle ring. If you cut farther from the edge, you will need to place holes or bails to attach to your piece. This clasp is meant to be as simple as possible; the hole for the toggle bar is also the point of attachment to the body of your jewelry.

Smoothing the cut sides of the circles before cutting out their centers.

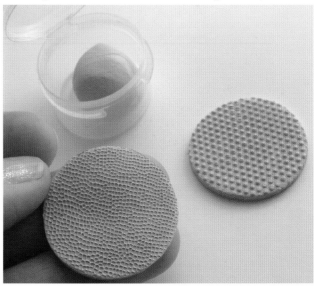

Adding a fine silver ring to a toggle bar is easy. Just pick it up on the U bail before you place the bail in the fresh, wet bar. Dry fully before firing.

3   Roll the cut-out from the center ring into a smooth ball and then roll that ball into a smooth, compressed cylinder, about as long as your circle clasp is wide. I generally make most of my clasps 1" to 1¼" (2.5 to 3.2 cm) around and my bars 1" to 1¼" (2.5 to 3.2 cm) long. Detail or texture the cylinder as desired.

You can easily form a curly-ended toggle bar by first rolling your cylinder about an inch longer than necessary, then rolling it down to points at each end. Quickly (because the clay is drying) roll the ends up into neat little curls. If the clay cracks or won't roll, you weren't quite quick enough from rolling to forming, or you used clay that was not fresh, or had already been over-handled. Sculptural techniques work best with very fresh, minimally handled clay.

4   Place the fine silver ring on the U bail. In one smooth movement, embed the ringed U bail into the rolled toggle bar. The success of your bar will depend on the quality of your embed. Don't just peck it into the surface. I like to flush-cut my U bails and then embed them all the way to the other edge of the cylinder, so that the two

blunt ends push the clay out into two nice-feely bumps on the other side. Imbed your own as much as you like, but be sure it's in at least halfway. If you don't push it in enough, and it falls out after firing, the only way to re-attach it is with solder.

5   Fire both pieces fully, for two hours at 1,650°F (899°C).

6   Hammer both the ring and the toggle bar to work-harden them. The ring can be lightly hammered from both sides, using stroking blows with a chasing hammer, but the bar will need to be propped up against the flat of an anvil or block and hammered from a variety of angles. Don't forget the bail and ring. Keep in mind that the success of having strong fine silver structural components depends on work-hardening. Tumbling isn't enough since it only finishes the surface. (Think of your tumbler as a barrel full of mosquitoes, with tiny mosquito hammers.) You need to get your work between a hammer and anvil or block to really do the job right.

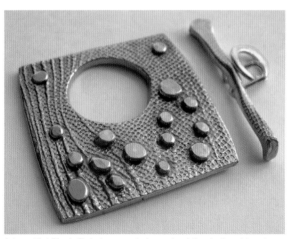

A beautiful Rivety Dot clasp made by embedding ball-end head pins, cut short, into a fresh square of textured clay and then hammered flat after the piece was fired and tumbled.

7   Buff, burnish, patina, polish, or tumble the finished clasp to taste. ■

Beads by
Joyce Rooks.

EAR WIRES | 2.0

Ear wires are easy and affordable to make yourself, and handmade wires always enhance a great pair of earrings. Their design also makes or breaks a pair of earrings—wires need to be the right size, weight, and length to complement their ornaments so that they hang properly in your ears and are not in danger of slipping out. You can bend your own ear wires quite simply around any round form, such as a pen, dowel, large round-nose pliers, or a Wrap and Tap tool, and you can use any type of wire that you like. If you use fine silver, as I do, don't go thinner than 18-gauge; it's simply too soft to hold up to wear in fine gauges. If you like very slender ear wires, consider niobium over sterling; it's nonallergenic, inexpensive, and an elegant metal, much like platinum.

MATERIALS

- Two 1½"–3" (3.8–7.6 cm) pieces of 18-gauge fine silver wire or other wire of your choice

TOOLS

- Flush cutters
- Round-nose pliers
- Wrap and Tap tool or a dowel, pencil, or other round form
- Chasing hammer and anvil or block
- Small metal file
- Tumbler

This technique is the simplest way to make ear wires, with just a turned loop, a rounded form, and longish legs. Make them both at once if you want them to be exactly the same. After forming your wires, remember to work-harden them with a hammer. Even if you don't want to forge the wires, you still need to hammer them for stability. If possible, tumble them overnight with stainless steel shot and a bit of dish soap as well. Ear wires and head pins are two components that benefit from long tumbling cycles.

1 Use round-nose pliers to form a small loop at the end of one the wires. Turn the wire around a round form, creating a classical ear-wire shape with your fingers. Hammer or forge the wire if you like (at least a little bit of hammering from each side is essential for work-hardening).

2 File the tips of the wire to make them more comfortable to wear, or tumble them overnight, or both. I always tumble my ear wires, because it helps to harden the wire as well as smooth any sharp cuts.

3 If you'd like fancier wires, ball, hammer, and pierce the ends of the wire.

To ball the ends of the wire, use a torch (see Drawing a Bead, page 135) or roll a small ball of fine silver metal clay, spear it on the end of the wire, and fire it at least 900°F (482°C) for one hour. (I use fine silver wire and so can fire at 1,650°F (899°C) for two full hours, allowing me to forge the fired ball as much as I like.) Hammer the ball or bead and pierce it with a hole punch or drill.

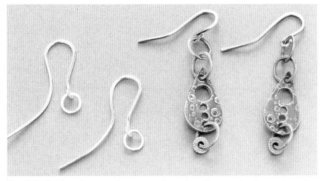

The light forging done on these ear wires gives them not only an elegant look, but makes them more comfortable for most people to wear. Leave the tails as long as you like to complement your design. Longer tails are less likely to fall out or need plastic clutches.

4 Attach a jump ring or fuse a fine silver ring to the wire. (See Fusing Fine Silver, page 137.) ■

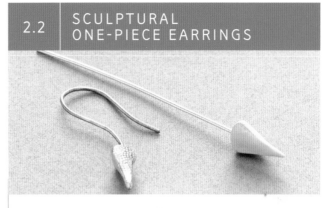

2.2 | SCULPTURAL ONE-PIECE EARRINGS

MATERIALS
- Two 3"–6" (7.6–15.2 cm) pieces of 18-gauge fine silver wire
- 5 g of fine silver metal clay

TOOLS
- Flush cutters
- Wrap and Tap tool or a dowel, highlighter marker, or other round form about ½" (1.3 cm) in diameter

These easy earrings are one of the most satisfying things to make with metal clay and wire. Simple sculptures speared on pieces of wire turn into a dramatic pair of earrings in just a few steps. As with the Sculptural S-Hook (page 10), the only other way to get this look would be to carve waxes for the sculptural ends, cast them, and solder on the wires. That's a fairly difficult job, but these adorable earrings can be completely finished in just a few quick sessions of work. Experiment with different sculptural shapes and lengths of wire.

1 Make two small sculptures of fine silver metal clay. Imbed one piece of fine silver wire in each of them.

Choose the gauge of wire based on what will fit through your or your client's ears; 18-gauge should fit most people and is thick enough to forge.

2 Fire the wires for one hour at 1,650°F (899°C).

3 Bend the wires around the round form to create the curve that will go through an ear.

4 Forge, patina, polish, and tumble the finished earrings to taste and until they are work-hardened enough for wear. ■

Bead by
Sarah Moran.

RING FINDINGS | 3.0

3.1 | RIVET POST RING

Beads by Joyce Rooks
and Sarah Moran.

MATERIALS

- 1½" (3.8 cm) of 12-gauge fine silver wire
- 5 g of fine silver metal clay
- 1 bead for the ring top that has a hole that will fit snugly on 12-gauge wire

TOOLS

- Flush cutters
- Flat-nose pliers
- Metal clay work surface, roller, texture sheet(s), and circle cutters or sharp craft blade
- Kiln
- Riveting hammer
- Chasing hammer
- Steel ring mandrel or anvil with a smooth conical horn
- Tumbler (optional)
- Patina solution (optional)

I love rings! They are the pieces of jewelry I wear every day and are reliable conversation starters, especially if they spin or are set with handmade beads. Making ring shanks in metal clay requires both full firing and aggressive work-hardening, but these two ring forms, a Rivet Post Ring and a Wrap Band Ring, are standards at my bench. Each can accommodate almost any ornament with a hole; beads, metal components, or found objects. They are both easy and versatile, open to many styles of ornament and embellishment. The Rivet Post is a permanent setting, but the Wrap Band can be easily reset, by just snipping the small curl of wire that holds a bead in place.

This simple and beautifully built ring is a snap to make out of metal clay and is a very sturdy base for your riveted treasures or spinny stacks. Imbedding rivet posts into metal clay and firing them into place is one of the techniques that I deeply value as a metalsmith. The traditional way to include posts in jewelry is to solder them on; a job that is not easy or enjoyable. Soldered posts are also not as sturdy as a properly embedded and fired wire; if you do a good job with your embeds, your fine silver posts will be permanently joined to your metal clay.

1   Roll and texture a sheet of metal clay to a finished thickness of 8–14 cards.

2 Use circle cutters or a blade to cut a ring shape. Keep in mind that the ring will shrink during firing, and you will be able to size it up after firing using a chasing hammer and a ring mandrel. Ideally, cut it to a size that is about a size too small after firing. That way your efforts to work-harden the ring will size it up just enough to fit you comfortably. As a guideline, an interior cut of 1" (2.5 cm) will fire to a ring size of about a 7–8. If you want a smaller ring, you obviously need to begin with a smaller starting size. To achieve a nice thick band and a size 8 ring, I usually make my outside cut 30 mm and my interior cut 25 mm.

3 While gently supporting the ring between your fingers, embed the piece of fine silver wire into the edge, pressing it all of the way through the clay until it bumps out lightly in the inside of the circle. Set the ring on a drying pad, trying not to jostle the embed at all. Don't pick the ring up until the clay is completely dry and even then, don't pick it up by the wire.

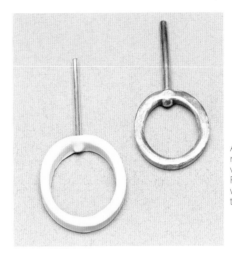

A fresh greenware clay ring and a fired, finished version ready for riveting. Remember that the ring will shrink about 15% in the firing!

5 Use a chasing hammer to work-harden the ring, then buff, patina, polish, or tumble the ring to taste.

Above, a greenware Rivet Post Ring, awaiting firing. Do not handle your embeds after they are placed. Let them dry on a kiln shelf and move the shelf to the kiln.

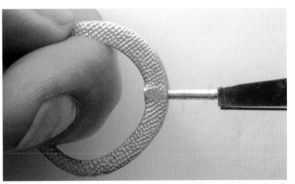

Straightening and work-hardening a rivet post: Use nylon-jaw pliers for straightening any gauge of wire and flat-nose pliers to get a good grip on the end of the wire, in preparation for twisting it a quarter to a full turn to harden the post.

4 After the ring is dry, fire it fully for two hours at 1,650°F (899°C). (Don't underfire or short-fire structural work such as ring shanks.) Work-harden the post by holding it firmly with flat-nose pliers in one hand while supporting the ring in your other hand, then pulling and twisting the post at least one full turn.

6 Rivet a bead or other element onto the wire. (See Riveting, page 133.)

This finding can be made smaller and used as a pendant bail as well. ■

3.2 | WRAP RING

MATERIALS

- 10 g fine silver metal clay
- ½"–¾" bead (1.3–1.9 cm) size of bead will determine the size of the ring)
- 2" (5.1 cm) piece of fine or sterling silver wire

TOOLS

- Large round-nose pliers or small Wrap and Tap tool
- Metal clay work surface, roller, texture sheet(s) and thin, flexible tissue blade
- Kiln
- Chasing hammer
- Anvil or steel block
- Tumbler (optional)
- Buffer (optional)
- Round-end burnisher (optional)
- Patina solution (optional)

Note: While this ring only uses about 10 grams of clay, you will need at least 25 grams of clay to achieve a large enough roll to cut out your form.

This clever ring form is cut from a sheet of textured metal clay and fired flat. After firing and cooling, it's gently bent around a steel ring mandrel or round form. Flat firing makes this a simple project to create in metal clay, and being able to bend the ring after it's fired will allow you to precisely size it to your finger. The size of the bead that you choose to ornament it will not only determine the look but the size of the ring; wider beads will spread the ring to a larger size. This finding works as a pendant bail as well.

1 Roll and texture a sheet of metal clay to a finished thickness of 6–12 cards. Cut a strip 8–20 mm wide and 3" to 3¾" (7.6 to 9.5 cm) long.

   Unless you are rolling out a fairly large amount of clay, like 50 grams, you may find it difficult to get a long enough piece to cut your ring out of. You may find it easier to get the right size of rolled sheet if you first roll your clay into a fat snake and then roll the snake into a sheet.

2 Use a small cocktail straw to cut at least one hole in each side of the strip to allow passage of the wire that will hold your bead (*Figure 1*).

3 Gently pick up the cut strip, being very careful not to stretch or pull any part of it. You don't want to thin the metal in the center, which is the spot that will take most of the stress of bending around the mandrel after firing. Carefully heal the cut edges with your fingers and place it upside down on a drying surface. Use a round-end burnisher to smooth the back side of the holes made by the straw. Allow to completely dry.

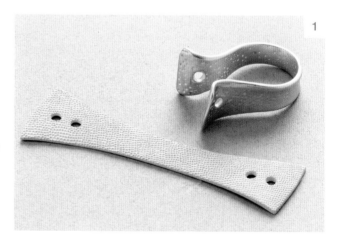

1

4 Fire the strip fully at 1,650°F (899°C) for two hours.
   This is a project that illustrates perfectly the need for
   full firing. If you underfire or short-fire this piece, it will
   simply break when you try to form it on the mandrel.

5 Gently bend the fired strip around a ring mandrel,
   supporting the strip at every stage of the bend. I have
   best luck when I hold the center of the strip firmly
   against the mandrel with my thumb and carefully form
   the rest of the shank around the barrel. Do not, under
   any circumstances, just pull down on each end of the
   strip. If you do that, the ring will form a V shape on the
   mandrel and will want to break at the center point.
   Support it completely, with pressure, as you bend.

6 When the strip is in a U shape, remove it from the form
   and curl the ends with large round-nose pliers or a small
   Wrap and Tap tool. If the ring is stiff and hard to form,
   stop bending and anneal it with the flame of a torch
   until it glows pink. Quench the ring in cool water. This
   process will make the metal become dead-soft again, as
   it was out of the kiln, and you can continue forming.

7 Work-harden the ring shank with a hammer and anvil or
   block and tumble it, if possible, overnight. Buff, patina,
   and polish the ring to taste.

8 Slide the focal bead on a short piece of wire and pass
   the wire through the holes of the shank. Use round-nose
   pliers to curl or bend the wire ends to taste, holding the
   focal in place. One advantage to this type of setting for a
   glass bead is that the bead can spin on the wire, making
   it less likely that it will break if you accidentally knock it
   against a hard surface. ■

STRINGING

Stringing with beading wire and crimps is often one of the first methods that people learn for making jewelry; it's quick, fairly easy to do, and when it's properly finished, beading wire will hold up well to wear. In the spirit of making all of your connections as smooth, functional, and as strong as possible, when choosing a beading wire or cable, select the thickest gauge that will go through your elements while still remaining flexible. Think of the wire as your support cable; you want it to be sturdy enough to hold the weight of your piece, but remain supple enough to allow for it to dance and move when you wear it. I choose the gauge of my wire and the weight and number of my crimps based on not only the size of the piece, but the length of wire between connections— longer spans are more vulnerable.

PROJECTS

- PUCK'S BRACELET
- DRAGONFLOWER BRACELET
- VICTORIAN BUTTON NECKLACE

Beads by Libby Leuchtman.

PUCK'S BRACELET

This playful and well-made piece has the feel of a much more complex structure. It has the lushness of a rope, a wide variety of colors and textures, and yet it's just a single strand! Elegant tiny silver true-cut seed beads cover the loops of beading wire for additional sparkle. Vary the elements of your bracelet to dramatically change the look of your piece. Change the pearls out for carnelian chunks, or the leaves for daggers. Use round glass beads instead of these unusual drops by Joyce Rooks. Pack your piece with vintage buttons! Let the constant in your strung work be attention to the detail of your connections.

MATERIALS

- Assortment of seed beads, including copper and silver size 11° true cuts and black and terra-cotta size 8°s
- 7 black/white/red/light blue 10x15mm lampworked drop beads
- 2 terra-cotta 8x6mm lampworked rondelles
- 1 gray/terra-cotta 8x6mm lampworked rondelle
- 1 carnelian 3x4mm stone rondelle
- 6 mauve 3mm freshwater rice pearls
- 1 green 5mm freshwater rice pearl
- 1 mauve 5mm freshwater potato pearl
- 1 bronze 6mm freshwater potato pearl

- 9 mauve 10mm freshwater round pearls
- 7 olive 8x12mm horizontally drilled glass leaves
- 1 orange 20mm resin flower with center hole
- 6 copper 6mm bead caps
- 2 Thai silver 3x2mm faceted rondelles or size 8° seed beads, to protect the two crimps
- 1 silver 11mm vintage glass button with metal shank
- 27 niobium-plated base metal head pins (substitution not recommended)
- 1 fine silver 9mm bead cap

- 1 fine silver 9mm fused ring (page 137)
- 1 fine silver 20mm toggle clasp (page 14)
- 2 sterling silver 2mm crimp beads
- 9" (22.9 cm) of bronze medium flexible beading wire
- 3" (7.6 cm) of sterling silver 18-gauge wire

TOOLS

- Round-nose pliers
- Flat-nose pliers (optional)
- Flush cutters
- Crimping pliers

PROJECT NOTES

Buy the best beading wire that you can; the cost of even the most expensive brand per piece is small. Invest in top-quality sterling silver crimps as well, as the longevity of your work depends on them. Each size of crimp tube has its own recommended pliers; to keep it simple, I stick with 2x2mm crimps and a single type of crimping pliers.

1   String one 10mm pearl on one head pin, form a wrapped loop, and set aside; repeat to turn 8 of the pearls into dangles (*Figure 1*). Continue by adding other pearls, the copper bead caps, seed beads, and small stone onto the head pins, creating 27 various dangles in all, including one that incorporates the resin flower. Choose to add one bead at a time, ornament some with a seed bead at the tip, or add several beads at once.

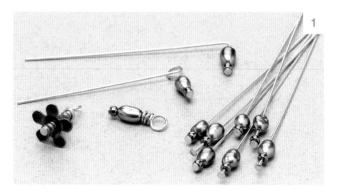

2   String one 10mm pearl on one head pin and form a wrapped loop that incorporates the 9mm fused ring. Set aside.

3   String 1 crimp bead, 1 Thai silver rondelle (or size 8° seed bead) 11 size 14°s, and the clasp ring on the flexible beading wire. Pass back through the rondelle and crimp bead. Check to be certain that the loop you create is large enough to move freely over the clasp ring. Adjust if necessary, then crimp (see Crimping, page 119).

   With the rondelle placed between the loop of beading wire and the crimp bead, your loop will be protected from rubbing against the sharp edge of the crimp every time you open or close the bracelet. Trim the tail wire at the crimp—there is no advantage to feeding the tail of the wire down into the beads.

I often ornament my loops of beading wire with 9–15 size 14° seed beads. Not only is it a classy look, sort of like French bullion, but it protects the beading wire from wear.

4   Set the second 8x6mm glass rondelle aside and string the rest of the dangles, lampworked beads, and glass leaves, interspersed by seed beads, along the wire in a pleasing pattern in the length of your choice (*Figure 2*).

5. String 1 crimp bead, 1 Thai silver rondelle (or size 8° seed bead) 11 size 14°s, and the 9mm fused ring. Pass back through the rondelle and crimp bead. Snug the beads, leaving a small amount of slack to allow the piece to easily flex into a circle, then crimp. Trim the beading wire at the crimp. Set the bracelet aside.

2

3

6. Form a wrapped loop (see page 122) at one end of the silver wire that connects to the toggle bar. String the bead cap and the remaining lampworked rondelle. Form another wrapped loop that connects to the 9mm fused ring (*Figure 3*).

Connecting your toggle bar in this way has several advantages—not only is your bracelet longer-wearing and easier to use, it's easier to size the bracelet up or down without ever having to cut the beading wire. All you have to do to make it bigger is to cut the wrapped looped connection securing your toggle bar and replace it with a longer connecting element (this can be done by switching the smaller rondelle for the larger blue bead, as shown in the photo). To make the bracelet smaller, replace the element with a plain wrapped-loop connection, with no bead.

I tend to make my strung bracelets small in length, knowing that I can easily size them up without having to cut the beading wire and restring the piece.

VARIATION :: USING A LOBSTER CLASP

A beautiful and inexpensive alternative to a handmade clasp is the simple sterling lobster clasp. Here, the strung segment of knockout pearls and seed beads is finished onto a simple soldered silver ring at each end. Add a charm stack onto one end and a sterling lobster clasp onto the other. The wireworked coils of the wrapped loop securing the lobster clasp to the bracelet was covered with a decorative square-stitched tube (see Square Stitch, page 115). This tiny tube is a lovely way to add the sparkle of seed beading to your strung work. Each little strip takes just a few minutes to make and adds mystery and interest to the piece. Think of it as ornament overlaid on top of your architecture. Some builders like their structure to show, others like to cover the bones of their connections with sparkle or frills.

DRAGONFLOWER BRACELET

The addition of felt balls makes this a fun piece, unexpectedly lightweight and textural. The soft felt is strung with herringbone-stitched flowers from the Ouroboros Bracelet (page 50), large vibrant freshwater pearls, and a vintage button. The addition of beading wire to the piece adds an element of sturdiness that thread alone cannot provide, and lets you build with components like tubular beadwork, which on their own are not good at holding structure. It's also an easy project to take on the go, as each component is separate, and can be made in about fifteen minutes. Make extra Ndbele flowers for matching earrings, and embellish an extra felt ball for a ring!

MATERIALS

- 1 g silver size 14° Czech true-cut seed beads
- 0.5 g silver size 11° Czech seed beads
- 2 Thai silver 3x2mm faceted rondelles or size 8° seed beads, to protect the two crimps
- 5 olive 14mm plain felt balls
- 5 mauve 7mm freshwater round pearls
- 5 olive/silver Ndbele flowers (see Ouroboros Bracelet, page 50)
- 1 bronze vintage 18mm button

- with a smooth shank
- 2 sterling silver 2x2mm crimp beads
- 1 fine silver 16mm toggle clasp (page 10)
- 9" (22.9 cm) of bronze medium flexible beading wire
- Size B or D nylon beading thread
- 1 clear 4 mm wide plastic drinking straw (optional)

TOOLS

- Flush cutters
- Crimping pliers
- Round-nose pliers
- Flat-nose pliers (optional)
- Size 12 English beading needle
- Sharp, slender beading awl

PROJECT NOTES

I enjoy making pieces with beady components, such as the Ndbele flowers, and often substitute gemstone rounds or lampworked beads for the felt balls in this piece. An advantage to the felt is that it's light as a feather on your wrist, and I love the added sparkle gained from encrusting the felt balls with tiny true-cut seed beads.

1 Cut the drinking straw into five 10 mm lengths. Set aside. This is an optional addition, designed to add a center support structure to the neck of each beadworked Ndbele flower.

2 Use the beading wire to string 1 crimp bead, 1 Thai silver rondelle (or size 8° seed bead), 19 size 14°s, and the toggle bar (*Figure 1*). (Check the fit of the loop of beading wire on your toggle bar or connecting ring, then adjust the number of seed beads up or down if necessary. You just want enough room for the loop to move freely.) Pass back through the rondelle and crimp bead and crimp. Trim the wire tail at the crimp. (See Crimping, page 119, for help with this job.)

3 String the button and 4 size 11°s. String 1 pearl, 1 straw section, 1 Ndbele flower, 1 felt ball, and 2 size 11°s, then slide the Ndbele flower down over the straw; repeat to add all the balls and Ndbele flowers.

   It's best to ornament the felt balls with beads after they are strung, so you don't accidentally break bead threads when piercing and stringing the felt. I was very careful to ornament the one in the photo and keep all of my threads to the outside rim of the ball, but it's much easier to just wait until the end to ornament them.

1

4 String 1 pearl, 2 size 11°s, 1 crimp tube, 1 protective bead (Thai silver rondelle or size 8° seed bead) 15 size 14°s, and the toggle ring. Pass back through the crimp bead, gently snug the beads, leaving a bit of slack so that the bracelet easily forms into a circle, and crimp. Trim the wire tail at the crimp (*Figure 2*).

5 *Optional:* Use 2' (61 cm) of thread and size 14°s to square-stitch (page 115) a strip 5 beads wide and 7 rows long. Wrap it around the final crimp and square-stitch the first and last rows together to form a beaded tube (*Figure 3*). Secure the thread and trim.

6 Anchor 1' (30.5 cm) of thread in one of the felt balls. Embellish the ball with size 14°s as desired. Secure the thread and trim. Repeat to decorate each felt ball.

A matching felt-ball ring on a Rivet Post Ring finding (page 18).

VICTORIAN BUTTON NECKLACE

Victorian shoe buttons, sterling silver chain, and handmade glass bring sparkle and excitement to a very practical hanging mechanism—a simple tube, covered in textural fine silver metal clay. Almost any type of attachment will work to make a tube into a neck piece; fiber, beading wire, chain, metalsmithing, or simple wirework. There are many different designs using covered tube that could be explored using the techniques in this necklace. I like the idea of cascading tubes, in graduated sizes, and I also like drilling holes in the tubes and using the drilled holes to hang or connect them. If you'd like matching earrings, short pieces of tube could be used vertically, with a few buttons hanging beneath them.

MATERIALS

- 56 brown/gray 9mm Victorian shoe buttons with metal shanks
- 114 Thai silver 2x6mm horizontally drilled bar beads
- 1 yellow/topaz 25mm or other lampworked flower donut
- 1 yellow/topaz 30mm or other lampworked flower donut
- 3" (7.6 cm) of sterling silver 7 mm tubing
- 5 g of fine silver metal clay
- 2 fine silver 14mm jump rings
- 2 sterling silver 7mm jump rings
- 9" (22.9 cm) of sterling silver 5x6mm chain, patinated to taste

- 6 sterling silver 2mm crimp beads
- 1 fine silver 16mm toggle clasp (page 14)
- 2' (61 cm) of heavy flexible beading wire
- 4¼" (10.8 cm) of fine silver 14- or 12-gauge wire (optional)

TOOLS

- Jeweler's saw (optional)
- Tube cutting jig (optional)
- Clay roller and texture sheet
- Tissue blade or craft knife
- Buffer (optional)
- Burnisher (optional)
- Tumbler (optional)
- Liver of sulfur (optional)
- Crimping pliers
- Round-nose pliers
- Flat-nosed pliers
- Flush cutters
- Torch (optional)
- Kiln brick or Third Hand (optional)
- Chasing hammer and anvil, or steel block (optional)
- Drill or hole punch (optional)

Lampworked beads by Sarah Moran.

PROJECT NOTES

You can either order a piece of precut tube (see Resources, page 140) or, using a jeweler's saw and a tube-cutting jig or clamp, cut a piece of sterling silver tubing to a length that works for your design. I covered my tube with metal clay, but you could use polymer clay, felt, fabric, or wrapped wire for equally interesting results.

1 Cover the tube with a very thinly rolled (one card or even less) sheet of fine silver metal clay (*Figure 1*). (See Rolling and Cutting Metal Clay, page 128–130, for help with this job.) *Note:* I find the easiest way to cover the tube is to roll the clay out to 3" to 4" (7.6 to 10.2 cm) long, place your tube at one end, and roll it up like a burrito, squeezing any air out. Use your fingers to pinch and squeeze the clay around the tube. Include texture on the final roll of the clay, if you like. If you cover your tube with a slightly thicker layer of clay, you can also carve it as it dries.

2 Fire the tube for 1 hour at 1,200°F (649°C). Buff, patina, burnish, and tumble it to taste.

3 Cut 5" (12.7 cm) of flexible beading wire. String 2 silver bars, 1 crimp bead, 1 silver bar, and one 14mm jump ring on one end. Pass back through the last bar and crimp bead and crimp. Trim the tail wire close to the crimp. Pass the long end of the wire through the silver tube. Repeat the stringing/crimping sequence on the other end of the tube.

4 Cut the chain into one 3" (7.6 cm) and one 6" (15.2 cm) section. Use a 7mm jump ring to connect one end of each chain to one of the 14mm jump rings (*Figure 2*).

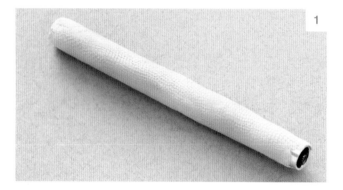

5 String the large donut on the short chain and the small donut on the long chain. Use a 7mm jump ring to connect the other end of each chain to the other 14mm jump ring.

6 Pass the remaining flexible beading wire through the tube. On each side of the tube, string {1 button and 2 silver bars} twenty-eight times. When you are sure the necklace fits, add 1 crimp bead, a protective bead such as a Thai silver rondelle or a size 8° seed bead, and half of the clasp to each wire end. Pass the ends back through their respective crimp beads and crimp. Trim the tail wires at the crimps (*Figure 3*).

3

Finished piece.

You can also connect the chain to the tube with a fine silver wire. First, cut a piece of fine silver 12- or 14-gauge wire to be 1" to 1¼" (2.5 to 3.1 cm) longer than your finished tube. Using a kiln brick or a Third Hand for support, draw a bead at each end of the wire. Hammer the resultant balls flat and pierce them with a drill or a hole punch. (See Drawing A Bead, page 135 for help with this job.)

Smooth the holes with a bead awl or file, place the wire through the tube, and bend the ends to form a U-shaped hanger. Place your large jump rings through the holes in your hanging bar to connect the chain and beads.

If you use beading wire, instead of balled, pierced, bent and forged metal, your piece will hang a bit differently, with a little more bounce.

BEADWORK

My first exploration into the world of jewelry design, and my first burst of engineering curiosity about jewelry, involved sewn beadwork. A friend gave me a cuff that she had made, handsewn with Czech glass beads and freshwater pearls, and I was hooked. It was built entirely of thread and glass; how, I wondered, could a piece of such gossamer be made to last? The thrill of discovery that I as a weaver could create a structure that was strong and supple remains with me today, and I continue to study beading and beadwork for a deeper understanding of how each pattern and thread path can be engineered to survive a lifetime of love and wear. Whether I am working like a carpet maker to edge bind my pieces or devising internal support systems for beaded tubes, I'm always thinking about the piece twenty or fifty years down the road, wondering how it will be holding up.

PROJECTS
- CORSET STITCH CUFF
- PEEP CUFF
- OUROBOROS BRACELET

- RIVERBED BRACELET
- FELT CUPCAKES
- FELT LEAF NECKLET

CORSET STITCH CUFF

This piece features a combination of square stitch and right-angle weave. The pattern is elegant and the weave is fluid and strong. Create the open "lacing" sections with one row of 2x2 right-angle weave and the bars and end sleeves with square stitch. Ornament the simple piece with a vintage button, sequins, or leave it plain and allow the delicacy of the weave to shine. The Corset Stitch Cuff features a fantastic engineering idea in action: a removable clasp allows you to easily reverse it, and prevents excessive wear at the closure. This design makes a very lightweight and comfortable choker, as well as a sturdy bracelet. For a choker, simply extend the piece to the desired length.

MATERIALS

- 10 g gold size 11° or 10° Czech seed beads (A)
- 5 g silver size 14° Czech seed beads (B)
- Size O nylon beading thread in color to match beads
- 1 flat shankless 30mm button (optional)
- 1 fine silver 20mm Ball-End Clasp (page 12) or Ram's Horn Clasp (see Resources, page 140)
- Beading wax or thread conditioner (optional)

TOOLS

- Beading tray
- Sharp scissors for trimming thread
- Several size 13 English beading needles
- Flat-nose pliers (optional)

PROJECT NOTES

This piece can be made in any width desired; just adjust the number of beads in your starting row up or down to taste. I began with a row of beads that contained 20 size 11° beads, spaced every second bead with a single size 14°, for a total of 29 beads. Near the end of the piece, I dropped down to 23 beads (16 size 11°s and 7 size 14°s) for the final four rows, creating a neat finish.

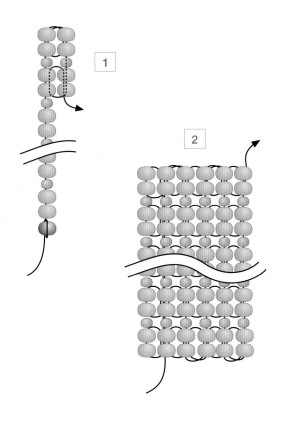

1 This piece is easiest to plan if you think of it as being assembled from four pattern pieces; two base strips, which will form the main body of the bracelet, and two 1" (2.5 cm) long square-stitched sections, which will become the end sleeves and will hold the clasp. You will sew one of the end sleeves closed when you have completed the pattern and leave the other open. As you will see, this is the secret to the reversible design and neat fit. To begin, use A and B to form the first of the two square-stitched and right-angle-weave base strips:

Row 1: Use 3' (.9 m) of thread to string a stop bead. String {2A and 1B} seven times and then string 2A for a total of 29 beads (or adjust for desired width).

Row 2: Square-stitch 2A to the final 2A of the previous row and pass through the next 1B, treating it as a spacer; repeat to the end of the row *(Figure 1)*.

Rows 3–15: Square-stitch 14 identical rows, reinforcing after every row. Keep the thread tension even and not too tight, but avoid leaving any looseness in the thread *(Figure 2)*.

Row 15, Unit 1: String 1B, 2A, 1B, 2A, 1B, and 2A; pass through the last 2A exited in the previous row, all the beads just added, and the next 2A from the previous row *(Figure 3)*.

Row 15, Unit 2: String 2A, 1B, and 2A; pass down through the side 2A from the previous unit, the nearest 2A from the previous row, and up through the first 2A of this unit *(Figure 4)*.

Row 15, Unit 3: String 2A, 1B, and 2A; pass through the next 2A from the previous row, up through the side 2A from the previous unit, the 4A added in this unit, and through the following 2A from the previous row.

Row 15, Units 4–6: Repeat Units 2 and 3.

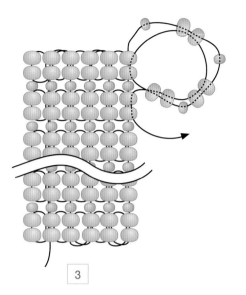

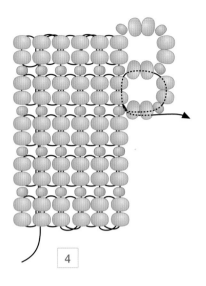

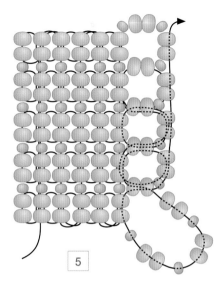

3

4

5

Row 15, Unit 7: String 1B, 2A, 1B, 2A, 1B, and 2A; pass down through the side 2A from the previous unit, through the 6A just added, and continue through the top A of every unit to exit from the top 2A of the first unit in this row *(Figure 5)*.

Rows 16 and on: Work square stitch as before off the top 2A of each unit in the previous row *(Figure 6)*.

Continue, alternating 3 to 6 rows of square stitch with 1 row of right-angle weave for a webbed look until you reach the desired length minus 1" (2.5 cm) for the clasp. Weave through the final square-stitched row to exit from the second 2A/1B set.

As you work, don't pull the thread too hard; keep the tension sufficient to avoid any loose threads. Reinforce as needed. I also chose to pass through each right-angle-weave unit at the edge again. I also reinforced every vertical row with a full pass before beginning a new row. When you reinforce like this, be certain to catch the tiny spacers with your thread. If you miss one, you'll see a thread crossing in your finished piece.

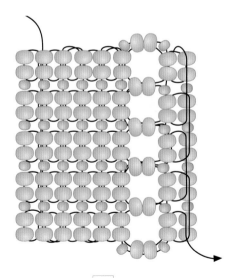

6

7

Final row: Work square stitch across the row in the 2A/1B pattern for a total of 8 sets, or 24 beads. Weave through the row to exit the second-to-last 2A/1B set. finish with square stitch.

2   Form square-stitched sleeves to attach the clasp:

Strip: Work a square-stitched strip off the end of the base in the 2A/1B pattern that's 6 sets wide and at least 12 rows long.
  I don't include the 1A in my stitches at the end of the row, but you may choose to do so if you wish.

Connect: Square-stitch the end of the strip to the last end of the base exited to form a ½" (1.3 cm) wide sleeve. Repeat the thread path as many times as possible. Keep in mind that if your bead holes are full, you can use the thread matrix to complete the reinforcement. Just dip your needle down through the beadwork and bring it back up through, catching a thread intersection on the way back up. Sew the two sides together as if you were hemming linen. Secure the thread and trim *(Figure 7)*.

Repeat this entire step at the other end of the bracelet base.

3   If desired, edge-bind your piece, with or without decorative accents. (See Edge Binding, page 118). You may also choose to sew a button to the base as a decorative element.

TIP	CHANGING THREADS

To change threads in this piece, which you'll need to do every 1" (2.5 cm) or so, weave the working thread through the finished work and weave a new thread in. Try to avoid knots in your beadwork.

Variations on the Corset Stitch Cuff. The beads you choose for your piece will drastically affect the design, as you can see.

VARIATION :: ALTERNATE CLOSURE

You can also leave your ends plain and sew on a hidden snap.

If you use a snap, sew it directly to the beaded fabric by accessing the thread matrix, not the bead holes, so that there is no disruption to the flow of the beads. If you cover the snap with a button, try to choose one with holes that match the holes in your snap, so you can sew the button on at the same time as one of your snaps.

PEEP CUFF

This cuff is a fluid and elegant piece, built entirely with square stitch, the simplest beading stitch I know. Its simplicity of design belies its elegance; it's intricate and sophisticated enough to wear to the opera. Like the Corset Stitch Cuff (page 38) and the variation of this project, the Mod Art Cuff (page 49), good engineering is in play—a removable clasp is employed both to add reversibility and to alleviate the stresses that come from sewing beadwork to fixed clasps. Complex patterns are easy to create when you choose to sew with precision-cut beads, such as the Japanese cylinder beads that the Peep Cuff is sporting.

MATERIALS

- 25–30 g green gold size 11° cylinder beads (A)
- 30–40 g rosy gold size 11° cylinder beads (B)
- 2–3 g pale gold size 14° three-cut Czech seed beads (C)
- 2–3 g copper size 14° three-cut Czech seed beads (D)
- 2–3 g gold size 11° Czech seed beads (optional) (E)
- 4–6 small freshwater pearls
- Black size B nylon beading thread
- 1 fine silver 1" (2.5 cm) Ball-End Clasp (page 12) or Ram's Horn Clasp (see Resources, page 140)
- Beading wax or thread conditioner (optional)

TOOLS

- Beading tray
- Sharp scissors
- Several size 12 or 13 English beading needles
- Flat-nose pliers (optional)

These pieces look lovely with the windows filled as well as open; you can suspend single pearls or stacks of tiny gems in them, or you can create them with color fields inside, to add depth or modern geometry. If you are planning on color fields, just add them as you sew, instead of building windows, and filling them in a second pass.

1 When I sew reversible cuffs like this one, in two layers, I work in one long swath and join the swath into a large loop. Then I close one end of the loop into a tube, or sleeve, to hold my clasp in place. There are no rules for assembly, though, and sometimes when I'm designing I'll make the main sections for the bracelet separately so that I can lay them on top of each other and see how they look together before committing to joining them in the piece. Do what's easiest for you; one swath or pattern pieces that you sew together.

To reverse the piece, just put it on upside down. The layers, only being sewn closed on one side, will self-adjust so that the piece lies smoothly on your wrist.

Reversibility can be used to full advantage when using color; you can create a totally different look by using very different colorways for each layer. This one reverses from a complex windowed piece to a simple stunning swath of sparkling gold.

This piece, like the Corset Stitch Cuff, is easiest to plan if you think of it as being assembled from four pattern pieces; two base strips, which will form the main body of the bracelet (Layers 1 and 2), and two 1" (2.5 cm) long square-stitched sections, which will become the end sleeves and will hold the clasp.

> **Row 1:** Use 6' (1.8 m) of thread to string 2B. String {1D or 1E and 2B} seven times so the row has a total of 23 beads.

> **Row 2:** String 2B and square-stitch them to the last 2B of the previous row. String 1D or 1E and 2B, then square-stitch the 2B just added to the matching 2B of the previous row; repeat across the row. At the end of the row, pass through the previous and current rows again to reinforce (*Figure 1*).
> *Be sure to reinforce after every row or your beadwork will gap and become fragile.*

Rows 3 and on: Repeat Row 2 until you've formed a strip 1¼" (3.2 cm) shorter than the desired length. Form a pattern by using alternating sized spacers, if you like. I mixed in size 11° gold spacers (E), which make the piece rougher and more textural, with size 14° copper charlottes (D), which slip quietly into the beadwork, leaving the weave completely flat.

Weave through the final row in Layer 1 and exit through the second 2B from the end.

2 Repeat Row 2, this time only working six 2B sets across for a total of 17 beads, to form a 1" (2.5 cm) strip off Layer 1; this is Sleeve 1. Use whatever spacer and cylinder beads you like. I used B and E for both of my sleeves (*Figure 2*).

Continue square-stitching 3 more rows, this time using A and C. Exit from an edge 2B

3 Square-stitch 2 strips and connect them to form Layer 2:

Strip 1: Work a square-stitched strip off Sleeve 1, this time only working two 2B sets across for a total of 5 beads (*Figure 3*).

Continue to work this thin strip until it extends the full length of your layer. Reinforce each row after it is completed. Set the working thread aside.

Strip 2, Rows 1–5: Begin a new thread that exits from the second 2B set from other edge of Sleeve 1, toward the center. Work a length of square stitch that mirrors the first 5 rows of Strip 1.

Strip 2, Row 6: Work 2 square stitches as in Row 3, then string {1D or 1E and 2B} twice. String 1D or 1E and pass through Strip 1's Row 4. Weave through the beads to exit through the inside 2B of Strip 1's Row 5 (*Figure 4*).

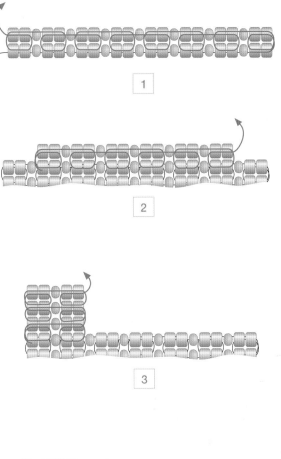

1

2

3

4

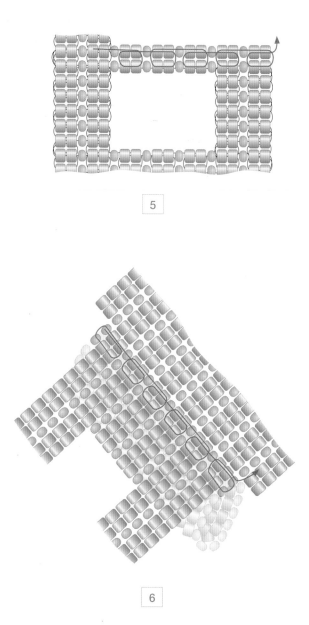

5

6

Strip 2, Row 7: Square-stitch across the previous row (*Figure 5*).

Strip 2, Row 8: Square-stitch across the previous row. Weave through the edge beads of Strip 1 and pass back through the previous row. Weave through the beads to exit from the first bead added to this row.

Rows 9 and on: Repeat Strip 2, Rows 1–8 to connect the strips, creating a second layer roughly equal to Layer 1. Depending on your wrist size, you may need to make it a few rows longer, to help the pattern work out. Make this layer longer, not shorter, than your widest layer, if your pattern forces you to choose.

4 Repeat Sleeve 1 off Layer 2, using whatever spacer and cylinder beads you like, to form Sleeve 2. I used B and E.

Gather the bracelet so Layer 1 rests on top of Layer 2. Test the bracelet for fit, keeping in mind that the clasp will take up an extra ¼" (6 mm). If necessary, adjust the length of the sleeves so that the bracelet will fit closely, but not tightly, on your wrist.

It's obviously easy to add more beads, but you might worry about how to subtract. Square stitch is actually sturdy enough to cut, so if you overestimated the size, you can simply trim a section out of a sleeve or layer and rejoin the cut ends with a square-stitched thread path, then reinforce the rows surrounding the repair.

5 Closure. When you're satisfied with the fit, square-stitch the final row of Sleeve 2 to the first row of Layer 1, and then sew one of the sleeves closed, forming a tube at one end. Make sure to leave enough room in this tube for the clasp to slide in and out, if you want it to be removable (*Figure 6*).

I like for my clasp to be able to slide out, but I don't want it to fall out, so I usually close my sleeve at a point where I will have to turn my Ball-End Clasp sideways to slip it in. Sometimes, if I'm sending a piece to a show or for photography, I choose to give up the idea of removing the clasp and will close the sleeve closely around the clasp so it can move freely, but so the sleeve is narrow enough that the clasp doesn't slip. This is a fantastic and long-wearing closure; the beadwork is not sewn to the clasp, but around it.

Important: Do not close the second sleeve into a tube, or your bracelet will not lay properly on your wrist!

6 Embellishment. If desired, ornament the sleeve closure with a layer of freshwater pearls, sewn through the weave of the fabric (not into the bead holes).

VARIATION :: MOD ART CUFF

A variation of the two-layer structure, the *Mod Art Cuff* is done in the same four pattern pieces, with sleeves of square stitch and, in this case, two layers of 2x2 right-angle weave forming the base. The different stitch makes for an entirely different look to the piece and allows the color of the base layer to peek through in a sort of pixilated pattern. This mixing of colors will add depth to your design and can be used to strong advantage graphically. If you enjoy embellishment, such as added layers of beads, sequins, buttons, or felt, the right-angle weave is a natural for accepting additions.

OUROBOROS BRACELET

Use herringbone stitch to create what would normally be fairly delicate tubes with flared dragon-wing ends, then engineer them for long wear by stringing them onto a sturdy beading cable. Choosing to string your tubular beadwork onto wire, cord, or cable is always a great choice. It avoids having to sew the beadwork to a clasp, and it offers the fun of the tube being able to turn, move, and slide as it's worn. Since the fact of the matter is that you are not going to be able to resist playing with it, it's your job as an architect to make this fun and fanciful bracelet with a structure that can stand up to the love.

MATERIALS

- 10 g copper size 11° Czech seed beads (A)
- 3 g silver size 14° Czech charlottes (B)
- 3 g red size 14° Czech charlottes (C)
- 32 copper iridescent fluted sequins (optional)
- 1 blue 10mm lampworked or other focal bead (optional)
- 1 fine silver 20mm toggle clasp
- 12" (30.5 cm) bronze medium flexible beading wire
- 2 sterling silver 2x2mm crimp beads
- 4 size 8° Czech round seed beads of any color or Thai silver beads with large holes to cover the crimps
- Beading wax or thread conditioner (optional)

TOOLS

- Beading tray
- Sharp scissors
- Several size 13 English beading needles
- Flat-nose pliers (optional, for pulling needles through beads)
- Crimping pliers
- Flush cutters

PROJECT NOTES

Herringbone stitch is easiest to begin by starting with a base row, or "ladder." I've shown it here with a ladder of four-bead square stitch. I find that single-row starts are too irritating to hold onto, so I generally do a two- or a four-bead ladder, which also makes a nice banded look at the start of a Ndbele flower.

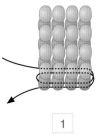

2

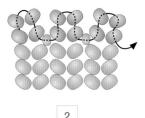

1

1 The body of the bracelet shown here was done with a width of 10 rows of beads, which equals 5 stacks of herringbone stitch. This stitch goes 2 beads by 2 beads, so you're always working with an even number of bead rows. I like to use size 11° beads for my tube and size 14° or 15° beads for my spacers, but of course anything you enjoy will generally work, as long as the spacers aren't larger than your tube beads. To begin, work square and herringbone stitch into a tube:

Base: Place a stop bead near the end of 3' (.9 m) of size B thread. String 8A; square-stitch 9 more rows off of these 8A, 4 beads at a time. Join the rows into a circle by sewing the first row to the last row. Reinforce the base by repeating the thread path at least once. Exit up through an edge A (*Figure 1*).

Round 1: String 2A, pass down through the next edge A on the base, and up through the following A; repeat around the circle to add a total of 10A. Pass up through the first A added in this current round to step up for the next and subsequent rounds (*Figure 2*).

Rounds 2 and on: Repeat Round 1 to form a 4" (10.2 cm) tube, or 6 rounds from your desired length.

2 See how the beadworked columns make a petal shape at the end of the tube all on its own? It's quite natural to add smaller beads, or "spacers," between these columns to create a flared, or dragon-like end. I find it works best to add these spacers in an orderly progression, one at a time as you stitch the round:

Round 1: Make a regular herringbone stitch by stringing 2A, passing down through the next A in the previous round, and then, before passing up through the next bead from the previous round, string 1B. Repeat this around to add 1B between each set of columns, creating an increase. Exit up through the first A added in this round (*Figure 3*).

Rounds 2–6: Repeat Round 1 for 5 more rounds, increasing 1A per round so that in the final round you're adding 6 spacer beads between each column.

If you try to add more than 6 spacers between the columns, the structure starts to get loose, like an old-fashioned umbrella clothesline (Figure 4).

Embellish: Decorate the flared end as much as you like, experimenting with different color combinations, thread tensions, and bead size differences. To form a double-flower-ended tube, as I made, you can either add the second flared end at the time you're securing the starting ladder or go back and add it to the finished tube after the first flared end is completed. Once finished, secure all the threads and trim. Set the tube aside.

3 Repeat the tube base, then repeat the flared end, this time using C as spacer beads. Secure the thread, trim, and set the flower aside. Repeat to form a second flower.

4 Use a crimp bead to attach one end of the flexible beading wire to one half of the clasp (see Crimping, page 119.) If you'd like, before you crimp add 11 to 15 size 14° beads to the wire, then make the crimp. Be sure to leave enough of a loop to move freely on your clasp.

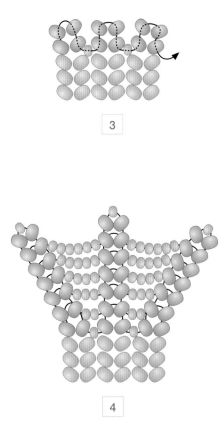

3

4

Bracelet elements.

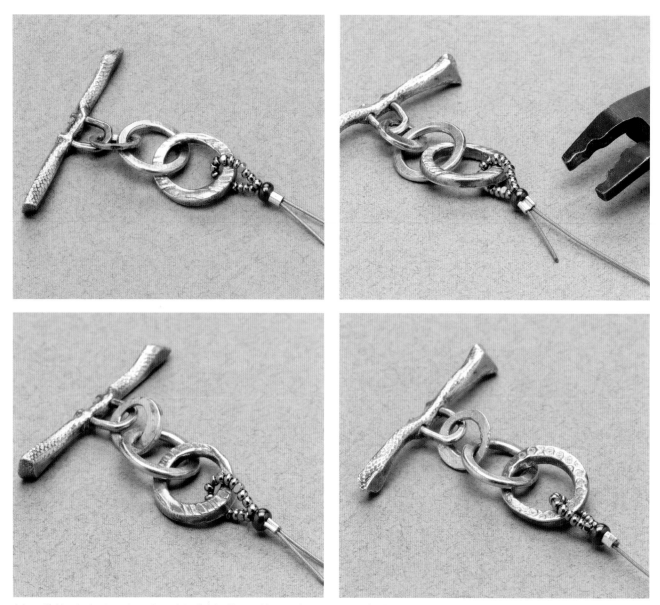

A beautiful beginning to a strung bracelet; a finished loop with enough room to move freely on the silver ring it's attached to and a neatly done crimp. Trim the tail of the wire right at the crimp—a few inches of tail will not help a badly done crimp and serves no purpose tucked inside the tube.

String the tube, both flowers, and the focal bead in a pleasing order. Use a crimp bead to attach the other wire end to the second half of the clasp. Trim that tail as well, right at the finished crimp.

Not tucking your beading wire into the adjacent beads is the secret to good crimping, especially a good second crimp on a piece. If you're not tucking the tail in, you can pull the wire out right behind the crimp and hold the tail and the body of the wire apart, so that the crimp can neatly bisect the wires. Tail-tucking will not allow you to do this properly (Figures 5 and 6).

5   If you'd like to sew the tube section of the bracelet flat, the best time to do this is after you string it so you don't accidentally impede the path of the beading wire with your sewing. To flatten the tube, simply pass through its side, between columns. String 1 sequin and 1B; pass back through the sequin and the tube to exit between the next two columns. String 1 sequin and 1B; pass back through the sequin and the tube to exit between the initial two columns. Repeat the fringe sequence, moving down the tube slightly with each stitch, to button the sides together. Generally, you'll only need to sew one side together; the piece will hold shape with that and there will still be a nice space left for the beading wire (*Figure 7*).

Think of the thread in your beadwork as a linen-weave fabric with lots of thread intersections. If you catch those intersections in a mindful way, you can sew your beadwork into any shape you like.

RIVERBED BRACELET

A sturdy square-stitched frame encloses a rippling sea of Victorian shoe buttons, vintage brass flowers, and pearls wired onto head pins. This piece offers a variety of clever engineering solutions to common problems with heavy and complex beadwork. The thread edges are bound after sewing, which not only protects them from wear, but adds another layer of horizontal structure, and the seed beads that are used as spacers in the weave also protect the vertical threads from coming into contact with the wired elements.

MATERIALS

- 5 g matte gold size 11° Czech seed beads
- 1 g metallic silver size 14 Czech seed beads (optional)
- 180–200 Thai silver or glass 2x4mm faceted rondelle beads
- 22 g rhodium-plated base metal head pins (see Resources, page 140; substitutions not recommended)
- 20–50 khaki, olive, gray, bronze, blue, and mauve 5mm to 7mm pearls with large enough holes for 22-gauge head pins
- 8–12 gray/brown 8mm buttons with wide metal shanks (optional)
- 10–25 dark rose 8mm metal, glass, or resin flowers with holes or shanks
- Black size O beading thread
- 1 fine silver ¾" (1.9 cm) toggle clasp (page 62)

TOOLS

- Round-nose pliers
- Flat-nose pliers
- Flush cutters
- Small sharp scissors
- Several size 13 English beading needles

See materials and instructions for Riverbed Bracelet's clasp on page 62.

3

4

Remember to reinforce every single square stitch on the rondelles with a second pass. This is critical to the piece. If you forget even a single reinforcing stitch, your bracelet will gap and sag, and will be very difficult to sew.

If your head pin eyes and/or flower shanks were larger than your size 11° seed bead spacers, they should ride smoothly on top of the row of four seed beads. If the shanks or wires are too small and get stuck in between the seed beads, your piece will not flow, and you need to either redo the embellishments to form larger eyes or restart your piece with a more slender seed bead. Not all size 11° seed beads have the same girth; the measurement only refers to their size from hole to hole, the idea being that eleven size 11° seed beads will stack up on 1" (2.5 cm) of thread; eight size 8°s fill 1" (2.5 cm), etc. The round Czech seed beads that I like to work with are among the stockiest seed beads made and require larger loops than the more delicate Japanese rounds.

After you stitch the second rondelle in Row 3 to its neighbor in Row 2, you should see how this piece works. The rondelles, each stitched securely to their neighbors, hold the piece together, the seed beads space the weave exactly and uniformly, and the embellishments ride on top of the seed beads, which neatly protect the thread from contact with the wires of the embellishments. Pretty neat! But it's important to have the ratios right, as you can see. If any of the embellishments get stuck between the seed beads, instead of riding neatly atop them, you will not only lose the flow of the piece and the separation of the metal wires from the thread, but you will affect the uniformity of each row because things that slip between beads add width.

Rows 4 to end: When you are satisfied that the elements are working together, repeat Row 3 to continue stitching and adding embellishments. This is what your piece will look like when you get 6 or 7 rows in place (*Figure 3*):

To add a button, string a button shank between the 2 center rondelles. If your shank is large, as mine was, add a seed bead spacer to sit inside the shank. As you can see from the photo, my button shanks spanned two rows of beadwork. Your buttons may only take up one row. Adjust as necessary for the fit of your elements and continue adding rows until your bracelet is long enough to fit your wrist, minus the length of the clasp. Secure the thread and trim.

3   Sew or use jump rings to attach the clasp:

Ring: Anchor a new working thread that exits from the first base row. Firmly sew the clasp ring to the edge of the bracelet.
   You'll need to find the most sensible way to attach your clasp; I designed my clasp (see Garden Gate Clasp, *page 62) so I could attach it to the end rows with fused rings, but your clasp may have holes or soldered-on loops, and you should accommodate them into your thread path in the most sturdy and sensible way possible. Choose a clasp with at least two attachment points to accommodate for the heavy weight of this piece (*Figures 4 and 5*).*

Bar: Anchor a new working thread into the other end of the base, test the bracelet for fit, and, if necessary, add (or cut off) a row or two of beadwork at the end before incorporating the bar or hook side of the clasp (*Figure 6*).

4   Edge-bind the bracelet (page 118), adding an embellishment of size 14° seed beads on the final pass, if desired. This binding will not only protect your exposed thread loops and offer an opportunity to decorate your edge, but it will allow you to even out the tension in your piece and will cover and even the tension in any areas you might have accidentally left a bit of slack.

GARDEN GATE CLASP

This lovely handmade clasp is built of fine silver metal clay and forged fine silver wire. You can choose to make a hook to close it, as I did, or you can construct a simple toggle bar (see Clasps, page 10.) Specialty clasps such as this one really make a piece your own, and building it out of metal clay gives you the opportunity to include specialty texture if you like and create it exactly to the size that would best suit your piece. Including a small bezel to fill with eggs, as I did, or a photo set in resin, can add an extra layer of interest to your work.

MATERIALS

- 25–50 g of fine silver metal clay
- 3 or 4 fine silver 8–12mm 14-gauge jump rings
- 1" (2.5 cm) of fine silver 10-gauge wire
- 1 fine silver 14-gauge ball-end head pin

TOOLS

- Metal clay work surface, roller, texture sheet(s) and thin, flexible tissue blade
- Small cocktail straw or other tiny hole cutter
- Round end burnisher or bead awl
- Small soft paintbrush
- Kiln
- Chasing hammer
- Anvil or steel block
- Round-nose pliers
- Craft blade
- Riveting or goldsmithing hammer (optional)
- Tumbler (optional)
- Patina solution (optional)

1 Roll and texture a sheet of fine silver metal clay to a finished thickness of 4–6 cards. (For my woody texture, I used a rubber stamp with a deep woodgrain.)

2 Use a sharp tissue blade to cut a gate shape. Mine is about 1" (2.5 cm) wide and 1¼" (3.2 cm) high with a gently curved top (*Figure 1*).

3 Using a stroking motion with your fingers, gently smooth the cut edges of the gate.

4 Use a cocktail straw to cut three or four holes (depending on how many rings you want to include) along one side of the gate shape. Use a round-end burnisher or bead awl to smooth the holes from the back side (*Figure 2*).

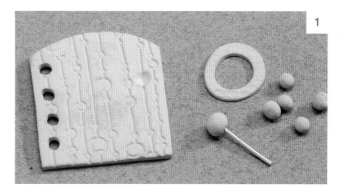

5 Trim the head pin so it's just long enough to embed completely into the front of the gate (about ¼" [6 mm]) and place it in the fresh clay as a doorknob (*Figure 3*). Do not manipulate the embedded head pin after placement.
Set the gate aside to dry to leather-hard.

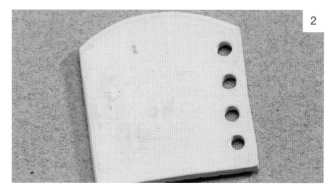

6 Roll five 2 to 4mm balls of metal clay and set them aside to dry. Roll a small amount of metal clay into a textured sheet 2–4 cards thick, and out of that sheet cut a ring shape about ¾" (1.9 cm) in diameter. Set it aside to dry to leather-hard.

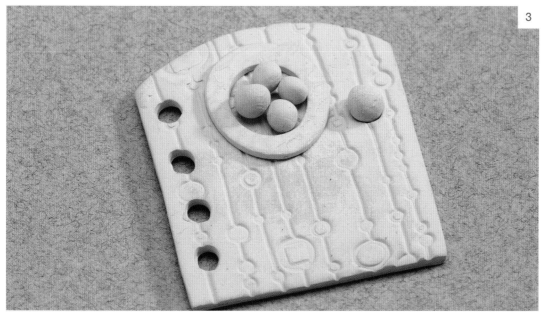

Gate formed before hole was cut for hook or bar.

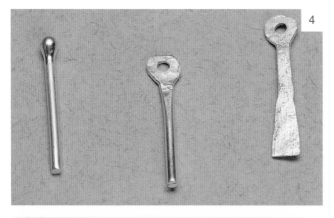

4

5

7 When the gate, ring, and rolled balls are all leather-hard, assemble the gate by using a soft clean paintbrush to lightly wet the top of the gate and the back of the ring with water. Place the ring on the gate. Allow the pieces to get just slightly sticky and then gently press and rub them together until you feel them grab. Use the paintbrush or a scrap of paper towel to clean up any extra moisture around the ring. Using a craft blade, neatly cut the slot for your toggle bar or hook.

8 Fill the ring with a bit of water or slip and drop in the dried rolled balls as eggs. Allow the balls to get sticky and gently press on them with your fingertips to seat them inside the ring. Allow the nest to dry completely. Recoat the balls and the inside of the ring with water or slip and allow the piece to dry again.

9 Using a wash of water, attach your signature disc to the back of the gate, if you have one. Set aside and allow to dry.

10 Form a toggle bar. You can do this with an embedded bail and ring (see Clasps, page 10 for help with this job). Or you could create a hook out of 1" (2.5 cm) of 10-gauge fine silver wire, by balling one end with a torch, hammering and piercing it (see Drawing a Bead, page 135), and then using the chisel point of a riveting or goldsmithing hammer to forge the other end of the wire flat (*Figure 4*). Use round-nose pliers to curl the forged end into a gently curved hook (*Figure 5*) and fuse or solder a fine silver ring into the pierced end of the hook (see Fusing Fine Silver, page 137).

11 Fire the bone dry clasp (and toggle bar, if you made one of metal clay) fully for two hours at 1,650° F (899°C). After the clasp is cool, work-harden it by hammering it gently on an anvil or steel block. Do the same for the toggle bar, if you made one, and then buff, polish, and patina to taste. Attach the clasp by including the rings in your beadwork in the most sensible way.

You might want to place the hook or toggle bar a few rows back so that the ends of the beadwork meet when the clasp is fastened.

FELT CUPCAKES

These little Cupcakes make everyone happy; they are soft and colorful and easy to make in just a few minutes. Experiment with different bead caps, types of chain, and color of seed bead or sequin to embellish the felt. Although I make a lot of unusual jewelry, I have to say that I get stopped most often when I wear the simple necklace of the four Cupcakes on the raw silk ribbon. They are oddly compelling, for such simple little treats. They also look wonderful in strung work, or as bouncy little ornaments on the ends of lariats, or pieces made with chain.

MATERIALS

- 4 felt 12mm balls
- 4 various-shaped vintage brass 10–12mm bead caps
- 4¼" (10.8 cm) of vintage brass 7x14mm decorative chain
- 0.5 g silver size 14° charlottes
- 0.5 g various-colored 14° charlottes
- 30" (76.2 cm) of rolled and sewn silk cord

TOOLS

- Size 12 English beading needle
- Size B or D nylon beading thread
- Sharp scissors
- Round-nose pliers (optional)
- Flat-nose pliers (optional)

PROJECT NOTES

You can cut felted wool easily with any sharp scissors, and you can add fibers, if you like, using either wet-felting or needlefelting techniques. You aren't limited to wool, either. I once washed a ball of golden-orange fur that I absentmindedly stuck into my jeans pocket after brushing my cat, Snicket. After the hot wash, I found a beautiful little golden felted ball in my pocket.

The blue felt ball is about to be attached to the chain link with a wrapped loop at the end of a sterling head pin. The others were sewn on with thread. Choose the method that works best for your piece. I generally prefer metal connections, as they are harder wearing.

1 Separate the chain into three 1" (2.5 cm) and one 1¼" (3.2 cm) pieces. Set aside.

2 Thread the beading needle with 1½' (45.7 cm) of beading thread. Anchor the thread at one end of a felt ball. Pass through a bead cap and a link at one end of one of the chain sections. Pass back through the cap and ball, string 1 seed bead, and pass through the ball, bead cap, and chain link again; repeat to take at least 12 more passes of thread, adding seed beads to the top of the ball and securing the ball to the chain as you go.

   You can also choose to secure the balls to the chain by piercing them with a head pin and using a wrapped loop to make the connection to the chain (see Wrapped Loop, page 122.)

3 If desired, add more seed beads to taste. Secure the thread in the interior of the ball and trim.

4 Repeat Steps 2 and 3 to make three more felt cupcakes.

5 String the felt cupcakes on a ribbon or cord or use them as components in your jewelry designs.

Lovely embellished flat or cupped felt flower shapes can be worn on ribbons, whipped up into eye-catching brooches, or made into fabulous rings. Here are two different styles of felt collage that I made; a flirty stack of precut flat flowers, embellished with seed beads and with a tidy strap band of seed beads on the back. Sew short bands to wear on ribbon and longer bands for ring shanks. Also, an elegant cup flower handmade by Gail Crosman Moore, with a few Felt Cupcakes (page 66) spilling out of the center and a snapped fabric ribbon loop that allows the flower to be added to chain, ribbon, buttonholes, hat bands, or anything else with a loop or buttonhole.

FELT LEAF NECKLET

This nifty project combines a variety of components and techniques to make an unusual piece of jewelry that will not only keep you warm in winter, but entertained over the years, as you switch components on and off of the leaf.

I love to embellish felt with beads, and you can see a variety of techniques in play in this photo. I've used free embellishment to randomly star the leaf with silver charlottes, an encrustation technique to stiffen and surround the golden felt ball in the center of the orange flower, and I've sewn a strip of right-angle weave and joined it around the tip of the leaf for a nice clean finish.

MATERIALS

- 4" x 8½" thick felt leaf shape
- 3 g silver size 14° charlottes
- 3 g matte gold size 11° seed beads
- 11" of vintage brass 7x14mm decorative chain
- 3 fine silver 20mm jump rings
- 1 fine silver 30mm fishhook clasp with connector ring
- 1 Felt Cupcake (page 66)
- 2 embellished flat felt flowers
- Sequins, tiny buttons, or other embellishments (optional)
- Flat fabric ribbon (optional)
- Sew-on snap (optional)

TOOLS

- Heavy-duty flush cutters
- Size 12 English beading needle
- Size B or D nylon beading thread
- Sharp scissors

I love to make pieces with interchangeable components and try to do this when working with any material. I particularly like the ribbon-and-snap system of changing lightweight ornaments on and off of this necklet, because it's so simple and long-wearing. Buttons are nice, too. You can sew a nice buttonhole or two in the felt leaf and create your ornaments with buttons on the back. Then you can simply button your delights on and off of your leaf.

1 Cut the chain into one 1½" (3.8 cm), one 1¾" (4.5 cm), one 6½" (16.5 cm), and one 1" (2.5 cm) segments. Use the jump rings to connect the segments back together in the order they were cut. Add a Felt Cupcake to the end of the chain with the 1½" (3.8 cm) segment.

2 Sew the other end of the chain securely to the stem end of the leaf. Sew the fishhook clasp's ring to the other end of the leaf, positioning the hook on the back of the leaf so the chain and leaf will lie comfortably on your collarbone (*Figure 2*).

I included the fine silver jump rings in my chain so that the necklace is easily adjustable; I can place the hook in either ring.

3 Sew the ribbon to the stem so it runs down the front center of the leaf. Embellish as you go by adding a size 14° seed bead to each stitch.

I sewed my ornamental ribbon to the leaf stem, but left a few inches loose so I could add a snap near the end. I can add components, such as Felt Cupcakes (page 66) or an embellished flat felt flower to the ribbon and snap it closed. Brooches, such as the small red flower, can be pinned to the leaf for further ornamentation. Change the components for a whole new look!

4 Embellish the leaf as desired, adding snap loops of ribbon to hold Felt Cupcakes, embellished felt flowers, or other adornments. Set aside.

5 Use 2' (61 cm) of thread and size 11°s to form a right-angle weave (page 117) strip 5 units wide and 7 units long, 2 beads per side, with size 14°s used as spacers. Wrap the strip around the leaf stem and sew the ends together to form a tube. Stitch the beadwork in place (*Figures 5a, 5b, and 5c*).

Wear the Leaf Necklet alone, or adorned with any assortment of the other felt components you've created.

The hook is held to the leaf with three sets of sturdy stitches. This stitchwork can be covered with seed beads to disguise it.

WIRE AND METALWORK

I first moved into working with wire as a way to form closures and components for my beadwork. When fine silver metal clay came on the market in the late 1990s, I was excited by the possibilities and began working with it with fairly single-minded dedication. When I realized that I was missing some critical metalsmithing skills, and that those skills were vitally important to making good metal clay pieces, I learned traditional bench work and incorporated those techniques into my findings and frameworks. It was a natural evolution, driven completely by the need for more original and sophisticated settings and the desire to create pieces that would stand the test of wear and time. The projects in this section are all explorations of functional design; whether they are ancient techniques such as loops (page 122) or contemporary designs such as the Mechanical Chain (page 84), each has in common a straightforward approach to its engineering.

PROJECTS

- PEARL CLUSTER
- ANCIENT CHAIN WITH RECYCLED GLASS
- MECHANICAL CHAIN

- KALEIDOSCOPE SETTING
- COCKTAIL POD RING
- TREASURE BOXES

PEARL CLUSTER

The Pearl Cluster is a lively element that can be made into earrings or a pendant or can be used as a component in other jewelry. You can use any type of bead or ornament that can be captured on a head pin to create the dangles. Choosing beading wire for the structure allows for a long-wearing piece that still has plenty of movement. If you were to gather the elements on metal wire, for example, instead of the flexible cable, you would have a stiff sculpture, without movement of the individual pieces. This construction allows your clusters to dance and sparkle and makes them fun to play with on the end of a chain.

MATERIALS

- 25–50 various 4 to 6 mm freshwater pearls
- 1 g of size 11° seed beads (optional)
- 25–75 niobium-plated base metal
- 2" (5.1 cm) head pins (substitution not recommended)
- 5" (12.7 cm) of bronze medium flexible beading wire
- 1 sterling silver 2mm crimp bead
- 1 sterling silver 6 to 20 mm hanging ring

TOOLS

- Crimping pliers
- Flush cutters

PROJECT NOTES

These clusters are endless fun to play with, like tiny jeweled toys. Experiment with different beads and materials; make them without hanging rings and use the circles formed of the beading wire to string them on chain or try them out as beaded beads in a more complex jewelry design. Capture them in a Cocktail Pod Ring (page 92) or in the center of a glass flower.

1 Place 1 pearl on 1 head pin and form a simple loop; repeat to prepare all the pearls. Add a seed bead to the tip of the pearl if you like. I placed one copper-colored size 11° seed bead at the end of each of my head pins.

2 Use the beading wire to string the pearls and the ring. As you are stringing, place the ring at the wire's halfway point (*Figure 1*). That way, it will always be opposite of the crimp bead when the cluster is hanging.

3 String 1 crimp tube and pass the other end of the beading wire back through the crimp so that the tails are exiting in opposite directions (*Figure 1*).

1

2

4   Place the U-shaped section of the crimping pliers on the crimp bead (*Figure 2*) and gently pull the ends of the beading wire until the ring of pearls is sitting closely (but not too tightly) around the pliers. Squeeze the crimp, remove the pliers, turn the crimp 90°, and finish the crimp by squeezing it with the oval section at the tip of the crimping pliers. (See Crimping, page 119, for help with this job.)

5   Trim the wire tails right at the crimp bead. See finished Pearl Cluster in *Figure 3*.

3

ANCIENT CHAIN
WITH RECYLED GLASS

Use simple double-loop connections in sterling wire to connect elements for a timeless design that's built to survive. It's just as easy to envision this piece coming out of the ground in an Etruscan dig as it is to imagine it sparkling on a gallery wall. This type of construction, if done well, is almost indestructible. You need to be mindful of how you handle your wire, of course—any metal wire can be fatigued by overworking, but if you turn your wire professionally, and use a sturdy enough gauge, these pieces can last essentially forever and represent one of the most ancient forms of practical engineering in wire.

MATERIALS

- 16 fine silver 15mm textured rings
- 6' (1.8 m) of sterling silver 18- or 16-gauge wire
- 1 fine silver sculptural head pin
- 1 fine silver 25mm toggle clasp (see page 14)
- 17 olive 10–20 mm variously shaped glass beads

TOOLS

- Round-nose pliers
- Flat-nose pliers
- Flush cutters
- Chasing hammer and anvil or steel block
- Tumbler and patina solution (optional)

Beads by Bronwen Heilman.

WIREWORK STYLES

One of my favorite applications for the double-loop connection is to form claspless chains of lampworked beads, long enough to slip over your head. Several strands of handmade glass beads connected by patinated turned wire is a powerful presentation, and makes a beautiful sampler piece for a lampworker to display.

The style of your wirework speaks to the soul of your piece, and perhaps your soul as well. Is your work precise and tight or flowing and done in multiple layers? Do you use fine or thick gauge wire? Do you like it shiny and clean or deeply stained? Matte or polished?

If you are just beginning to explore wireworking, I'd suggest that you get a few spools of inexpensive wire to play with, like copper, brass, or steel.

To perfect your skills, experiment with different gauges of wire and number of wraps. After just a few sessions, you'll feel comfortable judging how much wire you will need to make certain loops, and you'll get a sense of how much tension you want to apply. When I work, I tend to keep a firm tension on the wire, and place each loop precisely next to the previous one.

1 Lay out all of the beads in a pleasing pattern, placing your toggle ring third from the end of the chain and your toggle bar at the other end. Use the head pin to place a single bead as an ornament on the final link of the chain.

2 Cut 4" (10.2 cm) of wire and form a wrapped loop that incorporates the first ring. String the first bead in your design and form another wrapped loop that connects to the next mm ring. (See Wrapped Loop, page 122 for help with this job.)

   The length of wire required to form each link depends on the size of the glass beads. Check one for size before bulk cutting extra lengths of wire for wrapping, or, if you are using a variety of sizes of embellishment, cut each length of wire to a custom size. Do not make loops that are too tight on your rings, as you will want not only to have movement at each link, but to have enough room to forge each wrapped-wire loop for a real handmade look.

3 Continue connecting the beads and rings to connect all of those in the design. Attach the toggle bar at the end of the chain.

   Placing the toggle ring mid-design like this makes it possible for your necklace to form a Y or lariat shape when worn. Better yet, if each ring is large enough to accept the toggle bar, your necklace will be most versatile, as it can be clasped at any point.

4 Lightly forge the loops of wire that connect the chain and tumble and patina to taste.

MECHANICAL CHAIN

This is an intermediate to advanced metal clay project. The simple but exciting handmade chain is made entirely of metal clay and fine silver wire, and all parts are connected during a series of kiln firings. Each of the ball-end wires moves freely, for fabulous movement and a playful feel. This piece, and others like it, represent an exploration I've made into interpreting traditional metalsmithing techniques in metal clay. When you are building chain, or other structures that have to hold up to a lot of wear, one of the most important engineering considerations is movement. The Mechanical Chain explores moving parts both as function and ornament.

MATERIALS

- 125 g of fresh fine silver metal clay
- 2' (61 cm) of fine silver 14-gauge wire
- 1 fine silver sculptural S-hook clasp (page 10)

TOOLS

- Clay roller and texture sheet
- Sharp, thin tissue blade
- Beading awl
- Toothpicks
- Flush cutters
- Digitally controlled kiln
- Tumbler
- Soft paintbrush
- Tweezers (optional)
- Fine sandpaper or emery board (optional)
- Chasing or goldsmithing hammer and anvil or steel block
- Patina solution (optional)

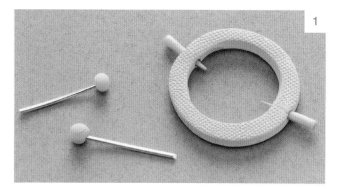

1 Roll and cut fifteen to thirty 25mm textured links and fourteen to twenty-nine 15mm links out of fresh fine silver metal clay, 12–16 cards thick. (Please refer to Rolling and Cutting Metal Clay, pages 128–130, for help with this job.) Set the smaller links aside to dry.

2 Form edge-on holes on opposite sides of the fresh 25mm fine silver links with a beading awl; insert a toothpick into the holes for firing. The toothpicks will burn out during the sintering process and the holes will be preserved.

   You could also choose to drill the holes later. Even if you plan on drilling, your job will be a great deal easier if you at least place pilot holes in the links and preserve them during firing (Figure 1).

3 Cut the fine silver wire into ¾" (1.9 cm) sections, enough to add two pieces of wire to each large link. Be very precise with your cutting if you want each ball-end wire to be exactly the same length; or vary the lengths to a pattern. Don't make them longer than your gauge of wire can support; you don't want them to be bendy. A ¾" length is perfect for fine silver 14-gauge wire.

4 Spear each piece of wire with one freshly rolled ball of fine silver metal clay, making sure that each ball is smooth before spearing it. Try to move very quickly to make each ball, as overhandling the metal clay will make the rolled balls crack. If you like a crackled look on your finished ball, then rolling them smooth is not an issue.

   If your rolled balls crack, don't worry—you can fix this later. After firing, use your metalsmithing torch to heat the finished fired balls to a red hot glow and then briefly flow the surface of each ball. The molten surface will flow into the cracks, resulting in a perfectly smooth ball.

5 Let the large links and ball-end head pins dry completely.

6 Fire the links and head pins in a digitally controlled kiln for at least one hour at 1,650°F (899°C).

   I would never underfire or short-fire metal clay chain structural or connecting elements like this if it were my final firing; these links and wires will go back into the kiln for another full firing when the chain is connected.

7 Use a bead awl to clean and ream the holes in your fired links or use a drill to enlarge them enough to not only accept the 14-gauge wire, but so the wires will be able to move freely in each hole. Tumble the wires and links to burnish and clean them before the final assembly.

8 Place a ball-end head pin through each hole in the large links and carefully spear the other end of each wire with a second freshly rolled ball of fine silver metal clay. Allow the finished links and wires to dry completely.

   If you don't have a lot of experience handling greenware clay or making metal clay chain, you might want to take this opportunity to fire all of your large links again so that all of the balls are permanently fused to the wires. This will make the links much easier to handle when you assemble the chain. If you do this, fire for at least one hour at 1,650°F (899°C) to set the balls (Figure 2, at right).

9 To connect the links into a chain, you'll be cutting the bone-dry, unfired smaller metal clay links and using them to join the larger fired metal clay links. Each of the large links should be ornamented with two ball-end wires. Use the blade to cut a wedge shape out of each small link (*Figure 2, at left*).

Your blade needs to be clean and sharp enough to cut the bone-dry clay with no chipping or damage to the link. If your blade cannot do this, it is either dull, or you have a thicker polymer blade. Tissue blades are very thin and flexible.

10 Place two large links on the smaller link and use a soft paintbrush to wash the cut section of the small link with water (*Figure 3*). Pick up the wedge piece with your fingers or tweezers and gently and precisely replace it in the small link.

11 Smooth the seams of the small link with the damp paintbrush. If your cuts were perfectly clean and your wedge piece went in the right way around (I actually use different texture on each side of my chain links to help me orient my cut pieces), then you should only see a tiny, fine seam at each end of the cut. A few soft strokes with your brush should heal all evidence of the joins (*Figure 4*). If not, let the assembly dry completely and refine the join with a piece of fine sandpaper or an emery board or metal file. If you need to file or sand your clay links, it's best to do it outside so that you don't contaminate your workbench with metal clay dust.

12 When you are pleased with the assembly and the cut links are completely dry, fire the finished chain fully for two hours at 1,650°F (899°C). The large links and ball-end wires won't mind second or third firings; you can heat your metal as many times as you like in the assembly of your pieces. Never underfire structural work; your chain requires a full firing to be solid and sturdy enough to forge.

13 After firing, hammer or forge each link with a chasing or goldsmithing hammer and anvil or block to work-harden them.

14 Buff, burnish, polish, patina, and tumble your finished chain to taste. Tumbling is very good for the ball-end wires, and is, in fact, the best way to work-harden them.

KALEIDOSCOPE SETTING

Very large disc beads are beautiful, but they can be a challenge to place in jewelry. This simple mechanical hanging mechanism is easy to make, and it showcases the beauty of the bead without distraction. The setting also allows the bead to move and spin, creating a kaleidoscopic effect. I'm quite pleased with this design; the size of the setting is easy to vary for different-sized discs; in the simplest version, it's just a longer or shorter wire. If you are adding things such as decorative discs, you can make them with pierced decoration or texture or ornament that matches the bead.

MATERIALS

- Large disc-style focal bead
- 4" (10.2 cm) of fine silver 12-gauge wire
- 1 fine silver ½" (1.3 cm) decorative metal ring

TOOLS

- Flush cutters
- Flat-nose pliers
- Round-nose pliers
- Chasing hammer and anvil or steel block
- Tumbler and stainless steel shot
- Torch and Third Hand or kiln brick (optional)

- Hole punch or drill (optional)
- Riveting hammer (optional)
- Patina solution (optional)

Bead by Tom Holland.

PROJECT NOTES

This type of setting can be done in several ways. The simple version shows it with just a ball-end head pin and a single ring, but page 91 shows the finished piece as a metalsmith would make it, with decorative front and back plates that are riveted closed and with a hammered and pierced drawn bead. Both are lovely.

1 Place an 8–12 mm ball of freshly rolled fine silver metal clay on the end of the wire to make a long ball-end head pin. Fire the head pin at 1,650°F (899°C) for at least one hour. Tumble the wire for several hours (or as long as overnight) to clean and harden it.

2 Bend the wire at a 90° angle, leaving enough room between the ball and the bend to comfortably fit the disc bead. Slip the disc bead onto the wire and use round-nose pliers or a Wrap and Tap tool to form a simple loop at the top of the wire (Figures 1 and 2).

3 Hammer the loop to work-harden it. Open the loop, slip on the decorative ring, and close the loop (Figure 3).

TURNED WIRE VERSION

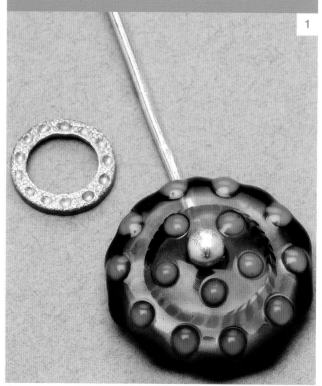

Bead by Isis Ray

1   Draw a bead on one end of the wire (see Drawing a
    Bead, page 135 for help with this job) and hammer
    it into a flat paddle. Use a hole punch or drill to
    pierce the paddle and fuse on a fine silver ring.

2   Bend the wire at a 90° angle, about 1" (2.5 cm) from
    the end, slip on a decorative back plate, the disc
    bead, and a decorative front plate. The hole on the
    front plate should match the diameter of the wire.

3   Trim the wire and rivet it at the front of the assembly.
    (See Riveting, page 133, for help with this job.)

COCKTAIL POD RING

This simple and elegant ring is embellished with a single pearl, set on an embedded wire post. This is one of my favorite projects in metal clay, as there is really no limit to how much you can vary the look of the piece. You can form your wire shank in any shape, with any type or gauge of wire, and you can allow the metal clay sculptural tips to stand on their own or hold settings, such as prongs. It's beautiful architecture, simple and clean, and it takes advantage of the best properties of both metal wire and metal clay. It's also a very strong form, as long as you remember to forge the wire shank for hardness.

MATERIALS

- 3½" (8.9 cm) of fine silver 10- or 12-gauge wire
- 1" (2.5 cm) of fine silver 8-gauge wire
- 5 g of fine silver metal clay
- 1 half-drilled 6mm freshwater pearl
- Clear jeweler's epoxy suitable for use with pearls

TOOLS

- String or strip of paper
- Kiln
- Ring mandrel, Wrap and Tap tool, or other finger-sized round form
- Round-nose pliers
- Flat-nose pliers
- Chasing hammer and anvil or steel block
- Small pearl drill or needle file to enlarge pearl hole (optional)

PROJECT NOTES

You can place any type of prong or embellishment in the fresh clay tips of this type of ring. If you want to set a half-drilled pearl, as I have, then you will only need a short piece of 18-gauge wire. If you want to set a found object, you can place several longer prongs, to wire-wrap around your treasure.

1 Use the string or strip of paper to estimate how much wire it will take to go around your finger. Add ¼" (6 mm) to ½" (1.3 cm) on each side to allow for room to sculpt the ends into a graceful form. Cut the 10- or 12-gauge wire to size.

2 Form two small fresh metal clay sculptures and embed one on each end of the straight piece of wire.
   I chose to make pyramids and embed the wire into their points. If you are handy with your fingers, you can choose to sculpt the metal clay a short distance up the wire at the base of each element. Beware of going too far with the clay on the wire, though; if you end up with a skin of clay in the area of the wire that is to be bent, it might crack.

3 Cut a ½" piece of 18-gauge wire and embed it into the center of one of the freshly sculpted metal clay ends. This will be the post on which you epoxy your pearl. Set the ring aside to dry completely.

4 Fire the dry ring for two hours at 1,650°F (899°C), and quench it or allow it to cool.

5 While the wire is still dead-soft from the firing, bend it around a ring mandrel or other round form into a shape that fits your finger and is sculpturally attractive.

6 Hammer or forge the base of the ring to work-harden and sculpt it. Buff, patina, and tumble the ring to taste.

7 Work-harden the prong by grasping it with flat-nose pliers, supporting the ring shank with your fingers, and giving it at least one full turn.

8 Use jeweler's epoxy to attach the half-drilled pearl to the prong wire.

TREASURE BOXES

Metal clay is ideal for box building and frame making because it's easy to attach dry slabs of clay together into almost any three-dimensional form you can imagine. When you plan your boxes, think of them as if you were designing small models of cardboard, with separately cut pattern pieces you will let dry and then assemble into finished forms. You can plan for boxes with lids that are hinged or riveted or simple open forms to hold photographs, beads, or to showcase found objects. Box building calls on your sense of architectural proportion, and your creations can be as complex and multidimensional as you like.

MATERIALS

- 25–50 g of fine silver metal clay
- Thin cardboard or paper

TOOLS

- Clay roller and texture sheet
- Sharp, thin tissue blade
- Kiln
- Chasing hammer and anvil or steel block

Bead by Dustin Tabor.

PROJECT NOTES

I make boxes that hold photographs, boxes with lids, boxes to hold beads, you name it. I love the box form in general and find endless fascination in the interplay of interior space vs exterior, of the idea of lids and doors, and I very much enjoy piercing my boxes with holes, whether windows in a building or portholes around a circular side. Your boxes can be perfectly smooth, mirroring those cut out of sheet at the bench and assembled with solder, or they can carry the texture of any material or surface you enjoy. You have a variety of finish options; you can stain them with patina, color them with colored pencil, decorate them with enamel, or any other surface treatment that makes sense for metal.

The easiest way to build boxes is to attach pattern pieces with just a wash of water and a little "squidging." This is called *drybuilding*, which is a term that differentiates forms or boxes built with just a wash of water from those assembled with slip, which is a slurry of clay and water.

1 Use the thin cardboard or paper to make a small model of your box design. You'll use these pieces as a pattern guide when you cut the clay.

   Remember that when you fire the box, it will shrink about 15%, so make your model a bit bigger than you want your finished piece to be.

2 Use the model as a pattern to cut pieces for your box from freshly rolled and textured metal clay, 4–6 cards thick (see Rolling Metal Clay, page 128).

To make the circular spacer, cut a flat strip of textured clay about 4 cards thick, and if you want windows in the strip, quickly (before it starts to dry) cut evenly spaced holes in the strip using a drinking straw. Harvest the

This is what your pattern pieces might look like for a round box with holes along the side. You can see my greenware pieces alongside a finished, fired version. This is a good illustration of the shrinkage from the greenware assembly to the fired box.

fresh clay out of the straw and roll it into your leftover clay. Bend the fresh strip into a circle and allow it to dry. I used one of the small plastic paint cups that I store clay in to dry this strip, and it gave me a circle about 26 mm in diameter, with overlapping edges. Use this overlap to cut a perfect join with a thin, sharp tissue blade *(Figure 1)*.

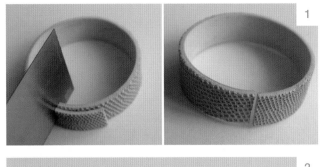

3   Join the circular spacer and the box parts together using a wash of water and a bit of pressure and movement. When you first slide wetted pieces of clay together, they will be slippery, but they will rapidly slow down, and you will feel them grab. At that point, the clay is bonded, and you can let the box dry before firing *(Figure 2)*. (As long as you keep squidging until you feel them grab, this is a stronger attachment method than gluing box pieces together with slip.)

4   When your forms are assembled and completely dry, fire the box fully for two hours at 1,650°F (899°C).

Box sides with holes are easy to hang on chain.

5 Use flat-nose pliers and a hammer and block or anvil to smooth or correct any warping and to work-harden the form.

6 Buff, burnish, patina, and tumble the finished boxes to taste.

7 Use epoxy resin or jeweler's glue to place beads, found objects, or photographs in the boxes.

If you prefer to include a bail directly in your box form, here is a nice way to do it. Place the bail ring in the box just like the other pieces, by wetting it and rubbing it until it grabs.

Bead by Dustin Tabor.

GALLERY

Over the years I've bought and traded jewelry that I found exciting or that featured engineering and design elements that I thought were exceptional. These are pieces from my own collection that I marvel over for not only their beauty but for the ingenuity with which they were crafted. From the settings made by Cynthia Archer that hold Amy Johnson's glass beads with such understated elegance and grace to the almost invisible shift in materials and structure that allow Teresa Sullivan's flame cuffs to morph from stretchy bead fabric to posable wired tips, I'm impressed by the creativity and technique that went into each of these pieces.

To the left, a stunning piece of jewelry by Cynthia Toops, who set the polymer cane moss mosaic in collaboration with Chuck Domitrovich, who did the metal work. Although Chuck's setting was cut and soldered at the bench, you could easily adapt the metal clay technique shown in the Treasure Box project to hold just about anything. This piece is very textural, almost alive.

Below, simple pendants I assembled out of favorite beads. Lower left, a large handmade glass bead by Dustin Tabor is set with double-looped connections in 18g sterling silver wire, on a fused fine silver ring. Lower right, two Frame Beads made by Michele Goldstein, each set with fine silver metal clay ornaments.

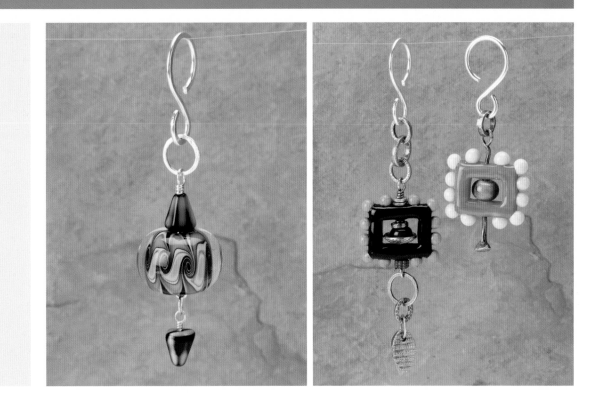

Clever fine and sterling silver settings by metalsmith Cynthia Archer hold handmade glass beads by flame-worker Amy Johnson of Tank Studios in Toronto. They collaborate under the name of Proper Jewelry, and these pieces were from their Bullseye series, done in 2005. I love the way the tube rivet holds each of the earring beads securely, but the prong frame is added both to balance the ear wire and to protect the setting from damage. The soft, square ring shank is not only comfortable, but easy to get on over knuckles that are larger than fingers. Each setting also allows the beads to be completely seen; brilliant!

The Tooth Fairy, a fanciful brooch by Kate Valleroy, of Red Anvil Studios. Kate's elegant combination of materials, a cow's tooth and a set of delicate silver wings, is a shock to the viewer, and her crisp attachment and sense of proportion impressed me technically. The size of the wings has everything to do with how this piece works. Kate is trained as a metalsmith, so she approaches all of her work with function irrevocably wedded to form.

Technically stunning earrings by Kim Van Antwerp. Handmade silver and gold TV-set settings, housing embroidered Godzillas breathing fire, set under vintage watch crystals. Handmade ear wires by Kate McKinnon. Tiny work is always impressive; the stitchwork is so fine that it must have been done with a magnifying glass. But what I really love about these settings is how seamlessly the different materials are assembled into finished pieces and how the detailing covers every part of the structure.

Rivet Post Rings (see page 18) by Kate McKinnon, set with a yellow handmade glass bird by Amy Johnson, of Tank Studios, an orange enameled disc from Objects and Elements, and a lavender and red handmade glass bead by Sarah Moran, of Z-Beads. The Rivet Post Ring is one of the simplest yet most effective designs I've created. It combines the immediacy and handmade nature of metal clay with the stability and durability of drawn wire. As you can see from these settings, almost any style or shape of bead can be used on the posts.

An unusual neck piece and ring. The neck piece is a collaborative design and features a crocheted rope of glass daggers made by Karen Flowers and a borosilicate glass focal bead by Gail Crosman Moore. The ring is a confection of wirework covered in bead crochet by Karen Flowers. Karen's signature is a tiny hot red bead at the tip of her work. I study these pieces for their engineering brilliance; Karen has taken simple bead crochet, which is not normally valued for durability, and made pieces that are clearly going to stand the test of time.

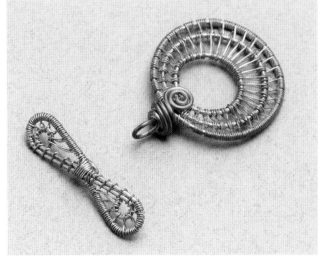

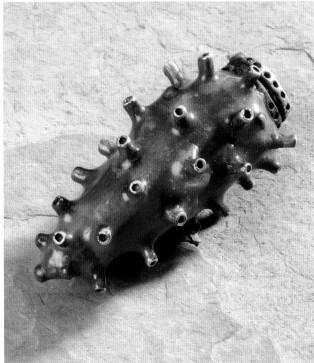

Above, Barb Switzer made this elegant and easy-to-use toggle clasp by looping and twisting fine copper wire. You can create components like this with a very simple set of hand tools and a round form. Barb's work impresses me not only for its precision, but for the care that goes into making sure that all of her connections are clean and well-engineered.

To the left, Kelly Russell made this richly colored amphora out of fine silver metal clay, with layers of glass enamel applied in separate firings. I love the way Kelly mimics tube with her rolled and partially drilled metal clay snakes. It would be almost impossible to discern simply from observing the piece what her processes were, and that fascinates me.

Flame Cuffs by Teresa Sullivan, which possibly repel bullets as well as looking cool as could be while they are at it. Teresa combined thread and wire to make these cuffs slightly stretchy, so they can go over the hands, and they are posable. They look stunning peeking out from under the cuffs of a suit jacket, and after owning them for four years, I am still marveling at their construction. The transition between sewn beads and wired is invisible; and the diamond shape of the sewn netting allows the cuffs to naturally flex to slip over my hands. Brilliant! All of Teresa's work is mindboggling; she is truly a bead engineer.

An intriguing carved polymer focal bead by Grant Diffendaffer, set as a pendant with fine silver by Kate McKinnon. This was one of Grant's early pieces. When I first saw his work I was struck by the thought and design skill that went into the way that he built his beads. He has continued to push the envelope of construction with polymer clay and has developed a series of structural techniques that cause many people to exclaim "This is polymer clay?" I always find it exciting when I study a piece and still can't say with certainty how it was done. This is a common occurrence when looking at Grant's pieces.

BASIC SKILLS

This section is included to show you the tools that I use every day at my bench and to provide instruction for techniques referred to in the book projects. The first section deals with tools, notions, and stitches for sewn beadwork, and the second addresses wirework, metal, and metal clay.

BEADWORK

The following basic tool kit is what stays with me for all tasks: beading, stringing, wireworking, and metalsmithing.

BEADWORK TOOLS & NOTIONS

WORK SURFACE. One of the lovely things about beadwork is how simple it is. For most projects, you don't need more than a needle, thread, a pair of sharp scissors, and some sort of tray to work on. Some of my beady friends work out of shallow wooden bowls, some use "design boards" with places to lay out strung work, but I just use stacking plastic trays, each one with a real velvet liner board inside. You can get the real velvet pads in a variety of colors from Fire Mountain Gems and Beads (see Resources, page 140) and the plastic trays from them or almost any jewelry display company. I love these because I can pick up my projects and carry them around (I bead in the garden, in waiting rooms, and on planes), and they stack so that I can have twenty-five projects going at once without it being a space problem.

From left to right, top: Two pairs of Swanstrom round-nose pliers, a Swanstrom flat-nose pliers, Wrap and Tap tool, nylon-jaw pliers, flush cutters, 2mm crimping pliers. *From left to right, bottom:* Nymo beading thread on the 3 oz spool, bezel mandrel, Thread Heaven conditioner, sharp scissors. All the tools are held in a nifty wooden tool holder, available from Rio Grande (see Resources, page 140) or any metalsmithing supply house. Missing from this photo is my bead awl, a slender pointed metal tool that I use for all sorts of things, and my Kemper round-end burnisher, both of which usually live in this box.

PLIERS. I keep crimping, round-nose, and flat-nose pliers on my worktable at all times. I usually don't need a chain-nose, but they can be handy for getting a grab in a tight spot. My favorite brand is Swanstrom, sold by Rio Grande (see Resources, page 140); I think they are the nicest, simplest, sturdiest pliers around, and they are offered in a 6" (15.2 cm) length that is very easy on the hands. One of their advantages is that they have a lot of torque. You may also notice very large round-nose Swanstrom pliers in my kit; these are for serious forming at diameters up to ¼" (6 mm). To go larger than that, I have Wrap and Tap tools, used for round forming and coil making.

I have nylon-jaw pliers, too, meant for wire straightening and for getting a good grab on metal without leaving a mark. I also have a bezel mandrel (the long round graduated cone) that I use for forming graduating jump rings or work-hardening chain.

CUTTERS. I always have a pair of nice sharp flush cutters on hand to cut wire. This type of cutting tool is flat on one side and V-shaped on the other so that I can make flat, or flush cuts.

SCISSORS. I use a pair of small sharp scissors to cut my beading thread.

BEADING NEEDLES. I prefer size 13 John James 2" (5.1 cm) beading needles. These are slender, flexible needles, which is what I need for delicately navigating the structure of my beadwork, for being able to slip in between beads, and for following contours. They are very thin, and some people find them difficult to see well enough to thread. I just pop on a stronger pair of reading glasses for the task. You can use a size 12 instead, for easier threading, but you will have less dexterity among the beads. My size 13 needles are easy to bend and sometimes they break; I go through several of them making each piece.

BEADING THREAD. For beading thread, I always use Nymo O, B, or D, in the three-ounce spool. These are available from Fire Mountain Gems (see Resources, page 140). Most bead stores carry smaller bobbins instead of the spools, and it's an entirely different thread. The Nymo on the spools is coated and lovely to work with. Get a spool of each size and you'll likely have a lifetime supply.

One of the things that I love about Nymo is the very thing that some beaders dislike; as you sew, previously placed stitches tend to grab the working thread, securing the new stitches in place. In this process, you might split the thread of those previous stitches, making it difficult to back out if you've made an error. I use this feature as a positive, and I deliberately place each new pass of thread directly into the previous stitches, so that the thread is woven into a fabric inside the bead holes, and the previous stitches hold the tension of each new stitch without pulling. To work this way, I have to slow down and check each stitch before I push my needle all of the way through. This has resulted in a mindfulness in my beadwork

that has led not only to a more peaceful experience, but to a better understanding of how the fabric formed by the weaving of the thread supports the structure of the beads. It was my first beading epiphany; that I, as a weaver, was responsible for the quality of the thread matrix inside my bead holes.

To back a stitch out that was placed this way, remove your needle from the working thread, gently pull out the stitch, rethread your needle, and repeat the stitch correctly.

I personally don't use any plastic beading threads or fishing line products, as I don't do tight work, and I worry about longevity. I'm not quite sure what fishing line will feel like in fifty years, but I'm fairly sure what silk and synthetics such as Nymo will do. I always protect my stitches, and in my beadwork projects you'll see techniques such as edge binding (page 118) and the insertion of clasps and rings in ways that don't damage the weave of the thread.

THREAD CONDITIONER. In the tray in the photo, you can also see a blue box of Thread Heaven, a thread smoothing synthetic wax. I sometimes apply this to my thread to keep it from fraying and tangling.

TOOL HOLDER. This nifty little wooden tool holder can be had from Rio Grande (see Resources, page 140) or any other jeweler's supply company.

BEADWORK TECHNIQUES

I have been seed beading now for about fourteen years, and I've spent a lot of time thinking about how to make better work. I've developed an awareness of not only the beads but of the thread structure that connects them, and I've come to think of that structure as equally important and valuable to the work. When I sew on a snap, a button, or any other surface embellishment, I'm generally not accessing the bead holes, but instead I'm using the linen-like weave of the thread that runs inside them. When I edge bind a piece (page 118) I'm not going through the bead holes again, but instead I am working like a weaver or a carpet maker, binding the individual stitches at the edge of my work into a sturdy cable.

Square stitch remains my favorite bead stitch. I love its structure, its sturdiness, and its willingness to accept many passes of reinforcement. I've come to love right-angle weave in the same way; it is willing to flow, to sculpt, and to stand at attention, depending on the intent of the maker. I'll occasionally use less sturdy stitches such as herringbone or peyote, but when I do, I generally choose to make tubes of it and give them a stronger central structure so that I don't have to ask those more fragile stitches to support a clasp or stand up to much wear.

You can see square stitch used to great advantage in the Peep Cuff (page 44) and the sewn sleeves at the ends of the Mod Art Cuff (page 49) and the Corset Stitch Cuff (page 38.) It holds an entire structure of rippling wired elements and seed-bead spacers in the Riverbed Bracelet (page 56), which is a variation of my popular Shag Carpet of Pearls piece. Right-angle weave is shown off in the body of the reversible, rippling Mod Art Cuff and the sexy vertical bars in the Corset Stitch Cuff. Herringbone stitch makes an appearance in my Ouroboros Bracelet (page 50) and the Dragonflower Bracelet (page 28).

I must admit that the most powerful tool in my arsenal for beadwork is patience. I've learned to slow down while I bead, to never tug my thread or pull it tight, and to check that each stitch is going through the correct beads before I push my needle all of the way through. Following are some helpful directions, courtesy of Jean Campbell, from her lovely book *The Beader's Companion*.

STITCHING BEADS. I work with beads in a variety of ways; I combine them with my metalwork, I string them on beading wire, and I sew with seed beads. People have the idea that seed beads are difficult to work with, but they aren't. A good pair of magnifying reading glasses and a nice cone of Nymo are all I need to enjoy hours spent weaving delicate slices of hollow cane into a rippling, supple fabric of glass. Here are three of my favorite beadweaving stitches, from the ground up.

SQUARE STITCH. Square stitch is my workhorse stitch. It's simple, sturdy, and can do anything. I use it to sew swaths of fabric and to make sturdy sleeves, tubes, and ladders. For the projects in *The Jewelry Architect*, I stitch the beads one by one, two by two, and also add spacer beads between the stitches.

Begin by stringing a row of beads. For the second row, string two beads, pass through the second-to-last bead of the first row, and back through the second bead of those just strung. Continue by stringing one bead, passing through the third-to-last bead of the first row, and back through the bead just strung. Repeat this looping technique across to the end of the row.

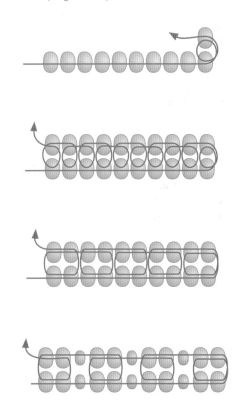

HERRINGBONE STITCH. Herringbone stitch, sometimes called Ndbele for the South African tribe that uses it extensively, is wonderful for the pattern it creates in the beads, but it's not a stitch that's easy to reinforce. I generally sew this stitch in one pass with Nymo D from the spool and use it for tubular pieces, where I can bypass its structural weakness by placing the tube over a core material such as beading cable.

Begin with a foundation row of square stitch (see page 115) a multiple of four rows long. Exit from the last bead along the edge. String two beads, pass down through the second-to-last bead in foundation, and up through the next bead. String two beads, pass down through the next bead in the foundation, and up through the following. Repeat to the end of the row. To end the row, loop around threads in the row below and pass back through the last bead strung.

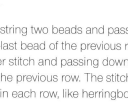

To begin the next row, string two beads and pass down through the second-to-last bead of the previous row. Repeat, stringing two beads per stitch and passing down, then up through two beads of the previous row. The stitching causes the beads to angle up in each row, like herringbone fabric.

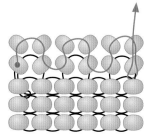

To make a herringbone-stitch increase, add 1 bead or more between stitches.

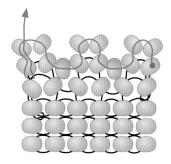

To form a tube, begin with a foundation round of square stitch so the beads lie horizontally. Exit from an edge bead. String two beads. Pass down through the next bead and up through the bead after it. Repeat around the tube. At the end of the round, pass through the first bead of the previous and current rounds to "step up" to the new round.

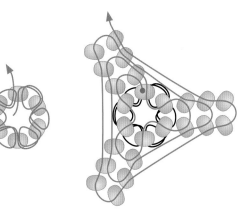

RIGHT-ANGLE WEAVE. Right-angle weave (also known as RAW in the beading world) is a sturdy, sculptural stitch that, like square stitch, can do anything. I love to use right-angle weave with two beads on each side of the little squares created by the weave so that the resulting open 8x8 cubes build a latticework fabric of glass, but the stitch can also be used very effectively with one bead on each side to form 4x4 cubes with almost no space showing. Right-angle weave is lovely for making tubular work as well.

To work RAW, string four beads and pass through them again to form the first unit. For the rest of the row, string three beads, pass through the last bead exited in the previous unit, and the first two just strung.

ADDING SPACER BEADS TO RIGHT-ANGLE WEAVE.

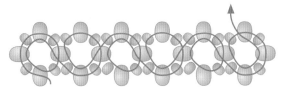

I add spacer beads to many of my stitches, including right-angle weave.

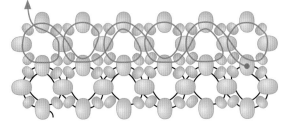

TIP

CHANGING THREAD THE EASY WAY

After working about 1" (2.5 cm) of right-angle weave, you'll find you need to start a new thread. When you notice your thread is getting short, leave yourself at least 3" (7.6 cm) and weave through the finished work, following the right-angle weave thread path. Avoid the edges of the work when weaving in tails, as you don't want any loose threads pulling out later.

Leave the thread end in place until you have your new thread started. While your needle is free, you might want to take this opportunity to weave in the tail of your starting thread as well. (Remove the stop bead on the tail, if you haven't already, before weaving it in.) You can trim both of those tails off as soon as your new thread is sufficiently anchored in your work.

Place another yard of thread on your needle, and, if desired, put a stop bead about 2" (5.1 cm) from the end. (Thanks to Valerie Hector for this excellent tip!) Insert the needle a few units back from your working space, weave through the beads to exit from the spot where you ended the last thread, take a pass through the final completed unit, and continue working. Once you've worked a new row, cut off the old threads and slide off the stop bead on your new thread and cut that tail, too. I always look forward to the first thread change, when I can begin to work tail-free.

To begin the next row, pass through the last three beads strung to exit the side of the last unit. String three beads, pass through the last bead passed through and the first bead just strung. String two beads, pass through the next edge bead of the previous row, the last bead passed through in the previous unit, and the last two beads just strung. Pass through the next edge bead of the previous row, string two beads, pass through the last bead of the previous unit, the edge bead just passed through, and the first bead just strung. Continue adding two beads at a time to complete the row, then begin a new row as before.

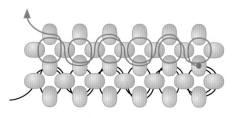

You can also work right-angle weave with multiple beads per side.

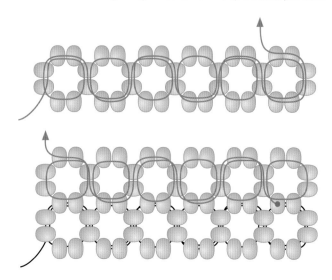

EDGE BINDING. Edge binding is a technique that I developed to protect the delicate thread loops at the edge of sewn beadwork. It is very similar to a binding that might be applied to a loom-woven work or a handmade carpet, with the intent being to wrap and gather the individual thread loops showing at the edge of a piece into a nicely wrapped cable. Embellishments can be attached directly to the resulting cabled edge, instead of you having to pass back through the bead holes to add things like fringe or a picot edge. Edge binding is also a handy way to move back several inches through a piece when it isn't convenient to begin a new thread to work in a nearby location. Also, if the holes of the neighboring beads are reluctant to accept more passes of thread, you can simply skip them, by edge binding your way along the clogged area, until you move into a zone in which the bead holes have more room.

To bind the edges of square stitch, anchor a fresh thread in your finished piece, move out to the edge at one end of your work, and pass your needle over and under the exposed thread loops at the edge. I generally make one pass in one direction, and then, when I reach the end of the piece, I turn around and make another pass back to the other end, which results in a nice double-helix sort of wrap of the edge threads. Pass through a row at the end of your piece, come out at the other side, and repeat the binding on the other side of the work. You will see a great difference in the finished edge of your piece.

If you like a delicate little beaded edging, you can pick up one or more seed beads on your second binding pass. If you like a fringed edge, you can complete the edge binding and then attach your fringe to the bound edges.

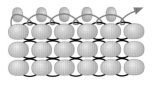

Binding the vulnerable edge threads of square stitch in this way not only protects them from wear, it also evens the tension in your piece and erases any minor errors you may have made, such as leaving a stray loop of thread or failing to sufficiently pull a set of beads together.

To edge-bind right-angle weave, anchor a fresh thread in your finished piece and take a pass through the bead holes, in a Greek key pattern down one side and then back up it, which will allow you to reinforce each segment of the edge cubes. Repeat this on the second edge. Stitches such as peyote and herringbone are very difficult to reinforce or to bind, and for that reason, I only use them to make hollow tubes, which I then fill with a stronger structure, such as cord, ribbon, beading cable, chain, memory wire, or rubber.

STRINGING BEADS. When stringing jewelry, I use Soft Flex beading wire, in either medium (.019) or heavy (.024). To close the wire, I use 2mm sterling silver crimps and crimping pliers, and I trim my wire at the crimp, instead of feeding it down inside my beadwork. This allows my finished crimp to be as professionally made as the one that starts my piece. Please see Puck's Bracelet, page 24, and Ouroboros Bracelet, page 50, for more details on how to include beading wire in your work.

CRIMPING. To properly finish a strung design, you'll want to use metal crimp beads to secure the beading wire. Crimping pliers are essential for this job, as they help create a long-wearing finish. If you just flatten crimp beads with a flat-nose pliers, the crimp won't hold up to wear as well as a neatly folded crimp does. Flat crimps are also sharper and will abrade your beading wire. Really good flush cutters are important to the job also, so that you not only cut the wire cleanly but at an angle. This will be helpful if you like to do things like thread on tiny seed beads to cover your loops.

You can see the assembly of the toggle bar end of my bracelet clearly here: a nicely sized loop with enough room to move easily on the ring it's holding; the beading wire of the loop covered by some size 14° charlottes; and a nice, smooth size 8° seed bead to protect the loop from the sharp edge of the finished crimp. This protective bead is crucial for long wear, as the edge of the crimp is the sharpest thing in your strung work. Do you really want it rubbing up against your structural loop every time you open or close your work? Any soft-edged bead will work in this position, and I sometimes use Thai silver cubes in place of the size 8° seed beads.

There are just a few important things to know about crimping. First, you need to leave enough room in your connections for things to move freely. Don't pull anything tight. Second, use a spacer bead between your loop and your crimp, as shown in the photo below. Third, your initial compression of the crimp (made in the U-shaped section of the crimping pliers) should neatly bisect your beading wire (*Figure 1*). The tail should be on one side, the working wire on the other. You can make sure this happens every time by holding the tail of the wire out as you squeeze the pliers.

Turn the crimp 90° and use the oval section of the crimping pliers to gently squeeze it together. Your goals are for the bead to neatly fold along your initial crease and for the lips of the crimp to meet neatly at the edge (*Figure 2*). You can squeeze the pliers all of the way down; the oval space is designed to make the crimp exactly right when it is all of the way closed.

Trim the tail wire right at the crimp (*Figure 3*). If you were taught to tuck it down inside your beads, trimming it so close might make you feel very vulnerable, but really, tucking that tail isn't going to save a bad crimp from coming undone. It offers nothing in the way of protection or stability, and it's just something to stick out and poke you later. Take a deep breath and cut it. Tug at your crimp. See? Sturdy. If not, you need to

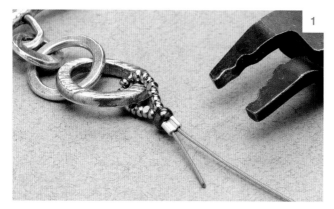

check to be sure that your crimping pliers match your crimp and that you are both cleanly bisecting the wire and folding your crimp all of the way over.

String on your lovelies, and then, when you're ready to close your second crimp (don't forget about the little protector bead between the loop and the crimp!) bring the tail of the wire out immediately after your crimp. Make sure that your piece has enough slack to easily form around your wrist or neck. As your tail is out, you can neatly separate the wires on your finishing crimp, and you can close it as professionally as you did in your starting crimp (*Figure 4*). Trim your wire immediately at the crimp. No tail tucking here either!

WIREWORK

Wire is a wonderful material. There isn't anything else like it in the world of metal. Wire is made by drawing a pour of metal through drawplates, which are blocks or wood or steel with graduating hole sizes. The wire is drawn down through progressively smaller holes until it is very dense. Making connections with wire is a wonderful way to build sturdiness into your work.

SIMPLE LOOP

A wireworking maneuver that I use regularly is that of the simple loop. It's not as sturdy as a wrapped loop (below), but is fine for many designs. Here are easy illustrations to help you do the job correctly.

WRAPPED LOOP

Wrapped loops are sturdy permanent loops that I often use for attaching toggle bars to my strung bracelets.

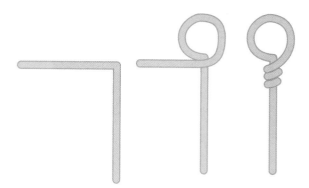

METAL CLAY AND METALSMITHING

Many of the basic skills used for fine silver metal clay can be found in my book, *Sculptural Metal Clay* (Interweave, 2010). Excerpted here are some helpful sections on tools, rolling clay, riveting, and fusing fine silver. If metalsmithing interests you, the entire book is packed with projects and techniques to take you further.

METAL CLAY TOOLS

I keep my workbench simple when I'm working with metal clay. I don't use additives or have any special unguents to keep the clay pliable longer. I don't buy any slips, slurries, extruders, oil-based repair goos, or extenders. I just use the metal clay right out of the packet and keep my clay from sticking to my tools and work surface with a very thin coat of olive oil. There are several tools that any metal clay craftsperson shouldn't do without.

WORKING SURFACE. I've seen quite a variety of working surfaces for metal clay. Some people use marked cutting mats, some choose glass or Plexiglass sheets, others prefer silicon or Teflon mats. I like a flexible work surface that can stand up to a blade, so I generally work on 6" (15 cm) squares of Teflon. You can buy Teflon in any cooking store; it's generally sold in sizes that will line cookie sheets or baking dishes. It's easy to cut down with ordinary scissors.

CLAY ROLLERS. To roll my clay, I use a tube of ½" (1.3 cm) PVC pipe cut into a 6" (15.2 cm) section. Some people enjoy using the metal tubes meant for making crepes, found in fine kitchen stores, still others prefer clear plastic or wood rollers. I like the PVC because it's cheap, slender, and doesn't stick to the clay.

A simple and inexpensive clay roller is ½" (1.3 cm) PVC pipe, with the cut edges sanded smooth.

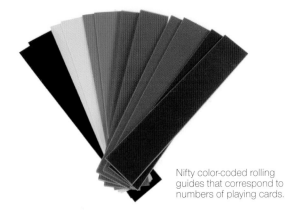

Nifty color-coded rolling guides that correspond to numbers of playing cards.

ROLLING GUIDES. Traditionally, metal clay artists have used stacked playing cards, set side by side about 3" (7.6 cm) apart, to form a width guide for rolling their clay. The clay is set in the center of the stacks, and when rolled, the resulting shape has a uniform thickness. So many people have been encouraged to use playing cards as rolling guides that many of my students still ask, "How many cards thick is that?", which is why I mention my rolling thicknesses throughout this book in the number of cards that my roll corresponds to.

To be honest, playing cards are dreadful rolling guides; they warp, compress, and get damp, and are too short to support a roll of clay long enough to make strap bands or ring shanks. So if you're serious about your metal clay work, don't use cards; choose firm guides instead.

You can make your own rolling guides out of metal slats, cut down to 6" (15.2 cm) lengths, or get yourself one of these nifty sets of color-coded rolling guides. I use these guides exclusively when I work, and it's handy because each one corresponds to a certain number of "cards." If you're an instructor, these color-coded guides are invaluable for helping your students easily understand how thickly you want them to roll and texture their sheets of clay.

RUBBER STAMPS + TEXTURE PLATES. I use rubber stamps, brass texture plates, and a whole lot of black rubber texture sheets to texture my clay. The stamps and rubber texture sheets must be oiled or sprayed with a nonstick coating before use. I like to use a light rub of olive oil for this because it evaporates cleanly from the stamps, never leaving them sticky. If you're using olive oil spray, which I love, never spray your stamps directly. Simply spray a bit on your palms, rub your hands together, and then rub the surface of your stamps.

A variety of cutters; clockwise: a four-petal flower from a cake decorating set, a one-inch round from a doughnut cutter set, three round Kemper Klay Kutters, and a professional Matfer pastry cutter.

Texture sheets and a large rubber stamp block.

CUTTERS. I use cutter sets and thin-walled pastry cutters with no seams for small shapes, chain links, and clasps and flexible 4¾" (12.1 cm) medical tissue blades to cut flat sheet, bevels, flat band ring shanks, box sides, and chain links. For cutting small holes or the centers out of small rings, I use a variety of cocktail straws and teeny brass cutters. I'll admit, I collect drinking and cocktail straws everywhere I go and become excited when I see a new one. Clean, sharp cutters will make all of the difference in making clean, sharp cuts.

Amazingly, at the time I write this, there are still no mass-produced professional metal clay cutters on the market. Especially lacking in our world are "donut" cutters; cutters that have a center punch to cut out a link or ring in one motion. It's very difficult to achieve precise center cuts by eyeballing them,

so as more professional jewelers play with metal clay, I imagine that the market will catch up with the demand for better cutter sets, especially if you join me in asking for them. Because most instructors don't emphasize the need for making clean cuts, many people don't know what a difference they can make.

MOLDS. I make texture sheets and molds with silicone molding compound. It's neat stuff that comes in two parts, like an epoxy. You use an equal amount of each to knead small balls together until they are an even color. You can then form patties for button-style molds or roll the compound out like clay to make impressions. When properly mixed, the molding compound is virtually indestructible after curing and won't stick to your tools or the metal clay.

SMALL PAINTBRUSH. It's true in every circumstance that the nicer your brush is, the finer your work can be. I like to use synthetic sable brushes, about ¼" (6 mm) wide, with bristles that are ¼" to ⅜" (6 to 9 mm) long. Invest in a nice brush or two. If you buy synthetics, you can get two for under $10. Nice brushes won't drop bristles in your work and don't leave brushstrokes behind.

OLIVE OIL. Olive oil is a great lubricant to use so your clay won't stick to your fingers and tools. It won't leave your tools or stamps sticky, as some sprays and balms will, but it can dissolve the clay and make a real mess, just like water. Don't use an excessive amount on your hands or tools. Spray your hands lightly with oil, rub them together, and then rub your lightly oiled hands on your work surface, roller, and nonsilicone texturing tools before beginning to work. Repeat as often as necessary throughout the work process. I generally oil a thing and then wipe it with a towel. This leaves a thin nonstick surface that won't add oil to your working clay. If you end up working too much oil into the clay, you'll change its chemical composition and may find the clay no longer workable.

STORAGE CONTAINERS. They're meant for holding leftover oil or acrylic paint, cost only pennies each, and seal completely to keep in the moisture. They come in two sizes to hold exactly ½ or 1 ounce (14 or 28 g) of metal clay each. Using these cups, I can keep opened metal clay fresh for months. I have no idea how I ever managed without them.

BEADING AWL. A slender, sharp probe, useful for reaming and cleaning holes or making pilot holes for later drilling.

PLIERS. I use four sets of pliers every day in my studio: a heavy-duty round-nose, a regular round-nose with long ergonomic handles, and two flat-nosed pliers, also with long handles.

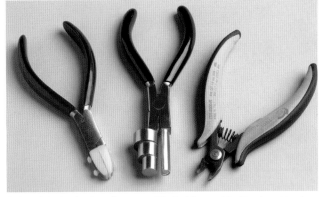

Left to right: A nylon-jaw pliers, meant for holding metal without marking it or for straightening wire; a Wrap and Tap tool, meant for forming curves or coils; and my favorite flush cutter. I now use this single cutter for everything I do at the bench.

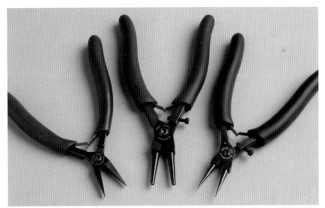

Three workhorse pliers from Swanstrom: a flat-nose *(left)*, a heavy-duty round-nose *(middle)*, and a regular round-nose *(right)*. These are my favorite pliers on the market.

Texture sheets made from two-part silicone molding compound.

Small plastic storage containers meant for paint hold exactly one ounce of metal clay in an airtight chamber.

WRAP + TAP TOOL. This ingenious hand tool provides not only a hardened steel barrel for forming or coiling wire, but a plastic-coated gripping jaw that won't mar your metal. Get the set of two, with three barrels each, for a total of six hard steel cylinder sizes in two easy-to-use pliers-style tools.

WIRE STRAIGHTENERS. The nylon jaws of this type of pliers are removable so they can be replaced when they get chewed up. I use these pliers not only for straightening wire, but for holding pieces that I don't want to mar.

FLUSH CUTTERS. I think I've bought every type of cutter on the market, but now just have one in my toolkit. It's crucial that your cutters be strong, sharp, and make perfect flush cuts if you want to fuse or solder your pieces.

BRASS OR STEEL BRUSH. I only use soft brass brushes on my fine silver work, although I know that many people have been taught to use stiffer steel brushes. I like the softer brass brushes because they don't rust, which allows me to brush my metal wet without being concerned about ruining my brushes, and because they don't stab me cruelly every time I pick them up. Brushes rapidly wear down and need to be replaced. I buy them by the dozen.

BURNISHER. Burnishers come in all shapes and sizes: some are long and resemble a beading awl, some are shaped like rounded scoops, and some are small handheld stones or pieces of metal harder than that being burnished. Pieces of agate are sometimes used to burnish greenware, with interesting effect.

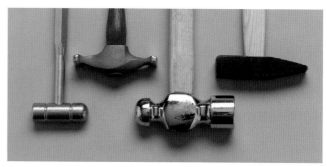

Four hammers *(left to right):* a small, lightweight brass hammer, useful for work-hardening bails and tiny chain links; a high-end texturing hammer; an inexpensive chasing hammer; and a nice 8 oz riveting hammer, perfect for fine silver. I could get by with only my riveting hammer or a nice goldsmithing hammer, if I had to choose only one.

SANDING PAPERS + CLOTHS. I don't do much sanding, but when I do, I generally prefer to use a small piece of very fine sandpaper or a salon board meant for synthetic nails. Each of these has a very fine grit.

TUMBLER. A tumbler is an essential tool for a metal studio; it can be loaded with many types of tumbling media and can easily clean an oxide surface or produce anything from a gleam to a mirror-finish shine on your silver. While I love large vibratory tumblers with easy reach-in lids, most home studios don't have room in their shops or their budgets for one. I don't. Instead, I use an amazingly inexpensive and sturdy rock tumbler. I fill my tumbler with 1 lb (0.5 kg) of mixed stainless steel shot, some water, and a little Dawn dishwashing liquid. I generally use it in 15-minute increments to clean and polish, or as long as overnight for ear wires, head pins, or rivets. A tumbler won't really work-harden your pieces, but it can produce a very clean and burnished surface on your metal.

HAMMERS. I use four different hammers in my everyday work: a small, lightweight brass hammer, for getting into tight places and for use on delicate pieces; a German chasing hammer, with a wide, flat round head; a heavy chasing hammer; and a chisel-point riveting hammer. Each of these has its place in my work and is chosen not only for head shape but for weight. The world is full of hammers; buy good ones and find ones that fit your hand. Most serious metalsmiths finish their own hammer faces by grinding and polishing to taste, but I admit that mine are straight out of the box.

Tumbler.

A slender bezel mandrel, useful for forming bezels, graduated coils, or for supporting small chain links in the work-hardening process.

ANVIL. I have a variety of anvils in sizes ranging from a little stainless steel 3" (7.6 cm) cutie to a massive 28 lb (13 kg) forming anvil with a long, curved horn. My workhorse anvil, however, is a 6 lb (2.7 kg) smoothly finished stainless steel anvil with a graduated horn. I'm also partial to my rough steel anvil, purchased for just a few dollars at a discount tool house. Each anvil or hammering surface has its own appeal, and I choose which one I want to use based on its weight, finish, and horns or holes. It would be difficult to get by with only one anvil.

RING MANDREL. Don't be tempted to skimp on this graduated tool used for sizing rings. Buy a good solid one, preferably with size markings carved into the barrel. If you set stones into your work, you'll want to have both a plain mandrel and one with a groove cut down the center to protect gemstone points while working the band of a ring. Ring mandrels come in shapes as well; you may enjoy using oval or square mandrels to shape your metal clay or wire ring shanks.

BEZEL MANDREL. I use a slender round bezel mandrel in spaces that my ring mandrel is too large to fit, such as inside chain links that I'm work-hardening or texturing, to wrap graduated coils, and to form cones. Again, don't skimp on this tool; it's a lifetime piece, so buy a good one.

A slender bezel mandrel, useful for forming bezels, graduated coils, or for supporting small chain links in the work-hardening process.

METAL HOLE PUNCH. I use a simple two-hole punch for my work—the two hole sizes are suitable for the majority of my punching needs. Punches come in all styles and sizes.

DRILL. I use a simple hand drill for most of my work, although sometimes, if I have a lot to do, I use a Dremel or a flexible shaft tool to speed the process. When I work with metal clay, I usually make my holes in fresh or bone-dry clay and have no need of a drill, although I sometimes use drill bits, and twist them by hand, to make tiny holes in leather-hard or bone-dry clay.

TORCH. I am devoted to my professional-quality handheld, portable, refillable butane torches. I do have a professional mixed-fuel Little Torch set up at my bench, although I admit that I rarely light it anymore; my butane torches can handle most jobs. I turn to my professional torch when I need a tiny, pinpoint flame, hotter than 1,800°F (982°C).

KILN BRICK. A kiln brick is an invaluable tool in a fine silver studio. It can be used for almost any fusing job or to draw large or petal-shaped beads on the end of wire. Kiln bricks can be purchased from most clay or kiln supply houses, are about the size and shape of a regular red brick, and can easily be cut with a wire or fine saw to your desired working size.

THIRD HAND OR TWEEZERS. Third Hands, locking tweezers, and protective fiber tweezers are all used to support or immobilize work in the flame. A kiln brick can, in most circumstances described in this book, take the place of the Third Hand and locking tweezers, because most fine silver work can be laid directly on the brick, with extraneous parts tucked away into channels dug in the soft brick.

METAL CLAY TECHNIQUES

ROLLING METAL CLAY. The basic techniques used when working with metal clay are what are known in the clay world as hand-building skills. Hand building is very different from wheel throwing because it rarely involves the use of water or slip for anything other than manual joinery on leather-hard or bone-dry clay, while wheel throwers use water with clay in all stages, and lots of it. Hand-building skills are used with every type of clay body, and many of the tools that we use to cut or manipulate the clay are the same as those you would find in a traditional clay studio. Making smooth balls, rolling and texturing even sheets of clay, and rolling snakes and coils are all methods you will use to do the projects in this book.

ROLLED BALLS + SIMPLE SHAPES. Perhaps the motion I use most as a metal clay artist is a swift, clean, compressive roll of a piece of clay into a smooth ball with no cracks. I use this technique to keep my clay fresh in its little container, but also to make and start many design elements or components. I also like to begin with a smooth compressed ball of clay before I roll a sheet of clay for texturing, as this helps eliminate problems associated with rerolling poorly joined leftover scraps of clay and the air bubbles that can result from careless handling.

Unless your design aesthetic involves cracked surfaces (which can be lovely) or you intend to sand and file each of your pieces (which, because I love you and want you to stay healthy, I don't recommend), you need to start each metal clay project smoothly to finish smoothly, so perfecting the cleanly rolled ball is key. Give yourself time to master this technique and don't give up; learning it is the best thing you can give yourself as a metal clay artisan.

The challenge is to achieve your desired form with as little handling as possible. Nothing dries the clay like your touch, so if you want it to remain malleable and smooth, it's up to you to touch it as little as possible. Your goal is to be able to pick up your clay scraps, firmly compress them between your palms, and then quickly roll them up into a ball or egg shape, all in about three seconds or less. The real secret is pressure, and lots of it, not a lot of rolling. I find that some people like to meditate on their next move by holding or rolling their working clay in their hands; these people also frequently have a problem with overdry clay.

This technique is important for a couple of reasons. First, when you roll sheets of clay, beginning with a smooth ball will produce a smoothly rolled sheet, free of air bubbles or cracks. Second, a smooth ball with no cracks, tucked away in an airtight storage container, has only one surface. Metal clay stored in this way—as opposed to just stuffed into the packet it came in as wads or scraps—will retain as much moisture as possible and, amazingly, can stay fresh for months.

Roll balls and eggs in various sizes, from the size of seed beads to the size of peas. Stack them up like tiny cannonballs and let them dry as is; these rolled balls won't go to waste. You can stick pieces of 18-, 16- or 14-gauge fine silver wire into the smoothest ones while they're fresh and fire them fully to make ball-end head pins. If you have a nice supply of both dried balls and fired ball-end head pins, you'll have lots of lovely choices to work with when it's time to build a little forest of silver fruit trees, a miniature rocky beach, a nest full of eggs, or a faux rivet. When you can roll a smooth ball of clay quickly and without effort, you are ready to handle the clay professionally.

Beautifully smooth rolled balls of fresh fine silver metal clay.

ROLLED BALL USES

Smoothly rolled balls of clay made into **HEAD PINS**; embedded in a **STACKED RING**; let to dry as little egg shapes and embedded in slurry and bone-dry clay pieces for a **NEST PENDANT** and a **PARK RING**, complete with boulders.

ROLLED SHEETS. It's important to practice rolling smooth, even sheets since you'll use this technique in almost everything you make from metal clay. To roll out, set two rolling guides (page 123) onto your work surface, one size (or two cards) thicker than your desired sheet thickness. Place the guides on each side of the clay lump. Use a roller (page 123) to smooth the lump into a sheet. Switch to the next smallest rolling guide size to roll your final thickness, or press or roll the sheet with a stamp or texture sheet (page 124).

If you'd like texture on both sides of your sheet, place the sheet between two textures and press or roll them both at once. It's important that your clay sheet remain even in thickness, so beware of thick and thin spots if you're working between two textured surfaces.

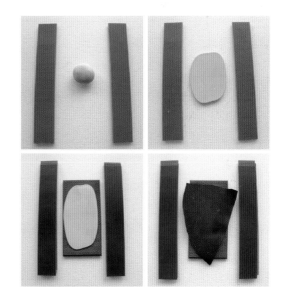

PRACTICE CLAY

If you'd like to practice rolling smooth clay balls or any other maneuver with fine silver metal clay, I suggest buying a small quantity of porcelain clay. The two clay bodies have much the same feel and dry and crack in about the same amount of time.

How to roll a textured sheet: First roll a smooth sheet, thicker than you wish your final textured sheet to be. Then place that rolled, smooth sheet between two texture surfaces and roll or press to create a smooth, even sheet with texture on both sides.

SNAKES. Snakes of clay are used either as a surface ornament, to strengthen the joints in a box form, or to fill a gap. Joint fills like this are used routinely in regular clay work, but rarely in metal clay because metal clay pieces are, in general, so small that the joins don't require support. However, if yours do, or if you have a gap to fill, a tiny rolled snake, pressed into the wetted bone-dry or hard leather-hard join or gap, and then smoothed with a tiny bit of slip or water, will do the job. You may enjoy using silicone-tipped watercolor blenders for this job (see Resources, page 140).

To roll a snake, place a smooth ball of clay on the working surface and lightly press it with your fingertips. Quickly move your hand forward and backward until the ball forms a cylinder of desired size and length. Never stretch or pull the metal clay. You don't want to build weak sections into your work, and pulling the clay does exactly that: it makes thin spots in the finished metal. If you want a longer or a thinner snake, roll it, don't pull it. As you compress and roll the clay, the snake will lengthen.

A simple circle, cut out of a rolled sheet of metal clay.

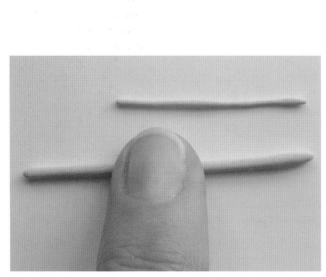

It's easy to roll snakes of metal clay with your fingertips to make toggle bars or tiny little snakes to reinforce box joins.

CUTTING. Cutting clean shapes out of rolled metal clay slabs is another important skill that many students aren't taught. When you use good cutting tools (page 124) and "heal" the cuts by gently stroking the edges, you'll have clean finished cuts without having to sand or file to get them.

It's best to texture your clay before you cut it, as you can distort your cut shapes if you texture them after cutting. In general, it's good practice to fully plan your pieces before you create them so you can make the most sensible decisions about rolling, texturing, and cutting.

Making holes in your pieces can be done at any stage. If you want extremely precise tiny holes in your finished pieces, drilling them bone-dry or after firing with a hand drill works well, but you lose the metal from the hole as it becomes dust on your bench. If you can work with slightly larger holes, they can be easily made in fresh clay with a tiny cocktail straw, then cleaned or reamed to size with a bead awl for a very precise look. Cutting holes in fresh clay offers the advantage of easily removing the bit of clay from the straw for later use. When I cut holes with a cocktail straw, I usually take that opportunity to roll the leftover clay into little balls and let them dry for later use.

SQUIDGING. If this isn't a real word, it should be. Squidging is firmly entrenched in the vocabulary of most clay artists because it perfectly describes the motion of using pressure while rubbing and worming a piece of clay onto another piece of clay, using the advantage of water or slip to make the surfaces sticky. Squidging is an active process, and the amount of pressure you use to move the pieces against each other will depend entirely on how dry and/or how fragile they are.

In traditional clay work, you'd score the pieces to be joined, apply water or slip, and then squidge the two pieces together. Scoring involves scraping or roughing up a clay surface to make it grabbier, but metal clay will not thank you for this. Skip the scoring and, in most cases, skip the slip. With metal clay, you can squidge leather-hard to bone-dry pieces together using just a small amount of water to bond their cleanly cut edges. Wet both areas of the pieces to be joined, wait just a moment for the clay to absorb the water and get sticky, then rub the pieces together, using as much pressure as is sensible. When you first move the pieces against each other they'll slip and slide, but they will rapidly get sticky and begin to grab.

To roll balls of the same size, use a cocktail straw or tiny cutter to cut the same amount out of an evenly rolled sheet of clay.

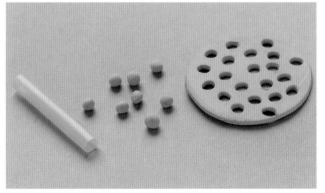

TIP — **FLOATING BALLS**

If you want the fine silver balls to appear to sit or float on top of the surface of a piece, don't use a dry-clay appliqué technique. Instead, embed short ball-end head pins, either made by drawing beads on fine silver wire with a torch (see Drawing a Bead, page 135) or by firing a metal clay ball onto the wire into your piece. Don't drop already fired balls into your wet divots. You may succeed in gluing the balls in place, but if you attempt to forge or form the piece after firing, they will probably pop right out. Finished metal balls can only be professionally applied to your metal clay piece by embedding them as ball-end head pins or after firing, using solder.

When they stop moving, they're bonded. At this point, take a damp, clean paintbrush and smooth the joint on each side. If you used slip, you'll probably have a bit of a mess to mop up. If you used a moderate amount of water, just a swipe on each side should do it.

You'll know if you haven't used enough water to squidge your join together if the pieces don't really slip and slide, or if you can't feel the active moment of grabbing. Practice joining pieces together at different stages of dryness, with different amounts of water, to understand the right balance of wet and dry for this job.

APPLIQUÉ. Appliqué is the technique used to ornament greenware (unfired metal clay) with other pieces of greenware. Using a little slip or water as a bonding agent, the clay bonds quite readily with other unfired pieces of clay at any stage of dryness. Water is sufficient for most appliqué; just wet both pieces and slip, slide, and squidge them together until you feel them grab. Don't just lay the pieces together and expect them

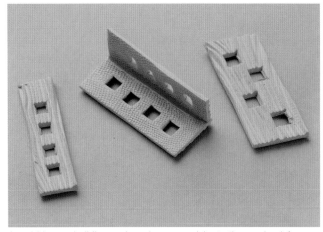

Assemble your buildings or box pieces one slab at a time and wait for each side to set up before you add the next.

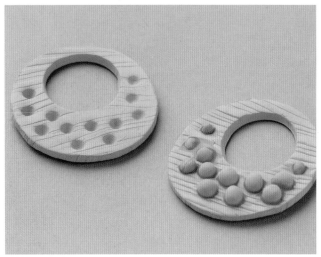

Smoothly rolled and dried balls of fine silver metal clay are placed in wetted divots, to seat them snugly in place. The finished, fired balls can be left round or hammered.

to bond, as if you were gluing. Making a permanent attachment, one that can't be knocked apart or easily broken, is an active process.

You'll find that some appliqués like to go onto bone-dry clay, some onto leather-hard. It's rare that you'd choose to appliqué when either piece is fresh and soft, but sometimes, when filling gaps or adhering to an uneven surface, the flexibility of fresh clay is just what you need to make a clean connection. Appliquéing dry balls to a fresh clay piece is a great technique to master. First, gently form small divots in the freshly rolled clay with a ball-end burnisher. Make your divots deep enough to fully seat the bottom of the dry balls.

To make divots in fresh clay without damaging a texture on the back side of your piece, let the piece air-dry for 15 minutes to an hour (depending on your humidity) on a sheet of Teflon, plastic, or glass, with the textured side up and the future divot side down. This will allow your divot side to remain fresh and soft, while the back surface with the texture on it air-dries. When the back surface is nice and dry, flip the piece over. The divot side, if it was snug against the Teflon, plastic, or glass sheet, should still be fresh and soft enough to place your divots, and the action of doing so will not damage the now-dry surface texture on the back.

Add a drop of water to each divot, just enough to fill it to the rim. Use tweezers to place a completely dry ball of clay into each divot, let the ball sit in the wet divot for a moment to get sticky, then press down on it gently. Rotate the ball a bit until you feel it stick in the clay. Mop up the excess water with a bit of torn paper towel or a cotton swab. Once the piece dries, the balls should be completely bonded in their divots. If you can easily flick off the embedded balls prior to firing, they weren't embedded properly in the first place. Each ball should be so well bonded that you should have to dig and pry them out if you want to remove them.

If yours aren't fully bonded, either your divots weren't deep enough to properly seat the balls, you didn't use enough water, or perhaps you didn't remember to press and roll them a bit in their wetted divots.

RIVETING

MATERIALS

- Fired metal clay pieces with holes
- Base with a fixed-rivet post

TOOLS

- Riveting or ball-end hammer
- Flush cutters
- Anvil with smooth horn or metal ring mandrel (or both)

Cold-joined rivets allow you to permanently connect two or more pieces of metal, through pierced or drilled holes, with a wire. This type of cold connection can be done with an embedded or soldered post or tube, which you flatten or flare at the ends to hold a collection of objects with holes together. You can also make a free rivet, a simple piece of wire with both ends flattened or flared. Rivets can be hammered down as tightly as you choose, to allow or not allow the items in the stack to spin. I generally choose movement for my pieces because things that move are more fun to wear, make people happy, and generate interest in the work.

1 Finish and patina the base piece. Pull and twist the rivet post to harden it (see Rivet Post Ring, page 18).

2 Stack the metal pieces with holes on the post, arranging them so there's no empty space. Make sure the hole of the top bead cap fits the wire snugly. It's best if everything in your stack fits neatly around the wire so that the post is fully supported, but a rivet can be done if at least the top layer is snug. If everything is floppy, you simply can't do a rivet.

If you need to fill the holes of any of the stacked items, consider using spacers such as tiny coils of wire, short cuts of metal tube, a stack of tiny metal rings, or large seed beads. If the top item in the stack has a filled hole, top the filled hole with a solid disc that covers the spacers to give you a solid platform on which to do your rivet.

A nice fired Rivet Ring Post Ring made with two bead caps and a spinny disc.

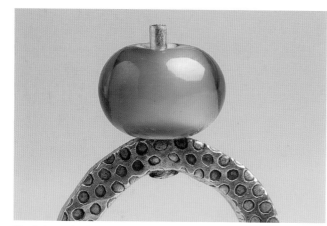

The first cut of a rivet post should be a bit high so that you can properly evaluate your final trim. (Bead by Joyce Rooks.)

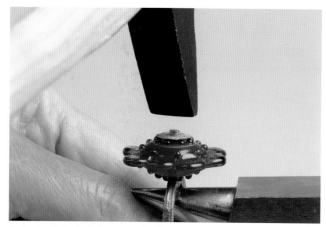

A shorter rivet wire being tapped with the chisel point of the riveting hammer to spread the top of the wire enough to trap the bead and the fine silver rivet angel but still allow the bead to spin. (Bead by Sarah Moran.)

3 Trim the wire, leaving less than 1 mm sticking up from the stack. This part is crucial: you'll be hammering this wire end, so you only want to leave enough to easily spread into a head size that will comfortably cover the hole. If you leave too much, it will want to bend instead of spread. If you leave too little, it won't be enough to spread out and cover the hole. Each rivet requires a judgment call about how much to trim, and your decision will be based on how tightly the items in your stack fit the wire and the gauge of the wire. If your holes fit snugly and your fine silver wire is nice and thick (like 12-gauge), you can leave as much as $\frac{1}{32}$" (1 mm) sticking up to give yourself a sturdy spread head. I usually try to come as close to that ideal as possible when planning riveted stacks in fine silver.

4 Support the base of the rivet post firmly on the horn of the anvil or metal ring mandrel. Hold the piece so the rivet post is completely vertical. Use the chisel point of the hammer to gently tap the top of the post. Turn the hammer or the piece, as necessary, to make sure wire spreads evenly. Keep the rivet post perfectly straight and go slowly. Many small taps are more effective than hard blows.

TIP	RIVET ANGELS

I often use my scrap fresh clay to cut out rivet angels: tiny flat spacers with very small pilot holes in the center. They help rivets happen easily by filling in larger holes or hugging wire more tightly than the underpinnings can.

DRAWING A BEAD

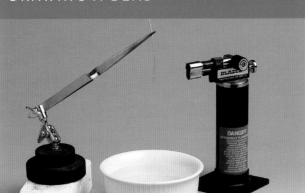

MATERIALS

- Fine silver wire in any gauge

TOOLS

- Protective tweezers or Third Hand
- Torch
- Kiln brick
- Wide-mouthed glass, ceramic, or stainless steel bowl filled with cool water, deep enough to submerge not only your hot wire, but the ends of your tweezers or Third Hand as well.
- Rimmed metal cookie sheet (optional)
- Metal hole punch or drill (optional)
- Tumbler + mixed stainless steel shot

This metalsmithing technique will come in very handy in your metal clay work. Drawing a bead is a skill that will allow you to make your own head pins, certainly, but can be used for decorative embedded prongs, hammered and pierced mechanisms, or any time you would like to use a wire but soften the end. The term "drawing a bead" is metalsmithing lingo for using fire to draw the molten end of the wire into a ball, or "bead."

1   Cut 2" (5.1 cm) or more of wire. If you want a shorter head pin, don't work with shorter wire; instead, cut it down after beading.
    For your own safety, don't use fire on loose pieces of wire shorter than 2" (5.1 cm). They are too easy to lose or drop, and one tiny piece of red-hot wire can start a fire or severely burn you.

2   Place the water-filled bowl next to the kiln brick. If you're working on a wooden tabletop or if you're just learning to work with fire, you may want to place all of these items on a rimmed metal cookie sheet for extra protection.

3   Use tweezers to hold the wire directly over the water-filled bowl. This is very important for your safety! As you're learning to do this technique, you may have molten balls melt off of the end of the wire and fall, so if you're over water, the quench bowl will catch them instead of your workbench, leg, or carpet.

4   Position the wire high enough so you have room underneath it for the torch. I often place the base of my Third Hand on a riser for this job. If you want the ball to be perfectly centered on the wire, keep in mind that you need to hold the wire straight up and down. Gravity is your friend, as long as you remember that it exists.

5   Turn on the torch and warm the wire for at least 1" (2.5 cm) above the spot you'd like to form the ball. When the wire is warm, but not red-hot, turn your torch so the tip of the cone of the flame directly heats the warmed wire tip. There will be a flare off the wire end if your flame is correctly positioned, and a ball of molten metal will rapidly form. If the ball doesn't form, your torch isn't hot enough, you're not holding the tip of the flame's cone exactly on the wire tip, or you aren't pointing the flame tip upward.

Warm the wire with your flame before you attempt to draw the bead.

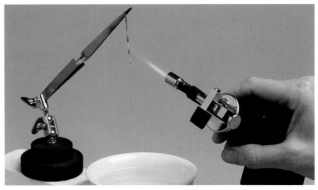

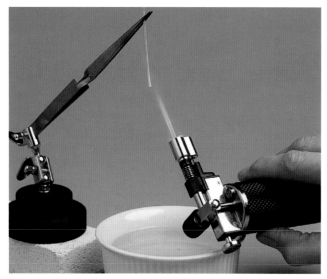

When your wire is warm, move your torch flame below the wire and use the tip of the cone of your flame to heat the very end of the wire.

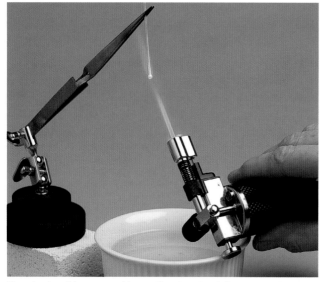

The wire tip will become red hot and begin to bead. Remove your flame when the bead starts to dance.

6　The gathering ball of molten metal will grow quickly and reach a point that it dances on the wire end. When you see the molten ball begin to dance, immediately remove the wire from the flame to allow the molten ball to cool. If you continue to heat the dancing ball without letting it set, the ball will drop off, potentially burning you or starting a fire. Drawing beads over a quench bowl is essential, even for experienced metalsmiths; sometimes there are weak points or flaws in a draw of wire that you can't see, which can result in unexpected separation of the molten end. Quench the entire wire and the tweezers or Third Hand tips (which will have become very hot) in the bowl of cool water.

7　To form a larger bead or metal ball, rewarm the wire shank and point the tip of the cone of the flame upward again, directly on the balled wire tip. There will be another flare off of the wire end. Continue heating and enlarging the molten end of the wire only until the ball dances again, then immediately remove the flame.

8　Once you're satisfied with your drawn bead, quench the assembly, including the tweezers or Third Hand tips. If you require a still-larger ball, you're best off making it flat on a brick or adding it with a rolled ball of metal clay and firing it in the kiln. There's a limit to how much wire can bead while suspended in the air.

9　Leave the resultant ball, or "bead," on the end of the wire as is, or forge it with a hammer and pierce it with a metal hole punch or drill for a jump ring or a fused, soldered, or riveted connection.

TIP	PETAL ENDS

You can make petal-shaped ball ends by drawing the bead flat on a kiln brick instead of suspended in the air. The bead will dance up the wire. You can then chase it with the tip of the flame cone until you're pleased with the shape. For a very large bead, take the flame away and let the wire and bead cool periodically as you move it up the brick.

FUSING FINE SILVER

MATERIALS

- 16-, 14- or 12-gauge fine silver wire

TOOLS

- Dowel or Wrap and Tap tool
- Flush cutters
- Two pairs of flat- or chain-nose pliers
- Kiln brick
- Torch
- Protective tweezers
- Bowl of water
- Rimmed metal cookie sheet (optional)
- Chasing hammer
- Anvil

Making chain is one of the real pleasures of the bench for me, and it's fairly easy to do by fusing fine silver wire rings. For this technique, you'll set already closed rings into a channel carved into a soft kiln brick, while you fuse the ring connecting them. This way you never have to bother with holding the assembly with tweezers or clamps while you fuse. This technique is not suitable for most soldering jobs because the solder flows to the base of a joint and relies on a completely clean and fluxed surface. The dust from the soft kiln brick would make a mess of the fluxed surface and might be caught by the solder flow as it is drawn into the joint. Fusing, however, relies on flowing the top surface of the joint of a pure metal ring, so doesn't drag any molten material along the bottom of the brick.

1 Wrap the wire around the dowel for as many revolutions as you need rings, plus a few more, to make a neat, tight coil.

2 Flush-cut the rings from the coil. Be sure to use good-quality cutters for this job because precise and evenly matched cuts are crucial for the next steps. Most cutters cut flush on only one side, so you will need to flip your cutter over between cuts, to make a flush cut on each side of the ring. You'll also need to be able to see the cuts and joins clearly, so wear magnifiers if necessary and work in good light. Poorly cut rings simply cannot be fused or soldered; there is no fix for a badly made joint.

3 Use two chain-nose pliers to neatly close 1 jump ring and place it on the kiln brick. You may wish to set your brick and quench bowl on a rimmed metal cookie sheet for safety.

4 Use the torch to either warm the whole ring slowly or focus the flame on the kiln brick in front of the jump ring's joint. Either method works well, but the latter will keep the surface of the ring more pristine, as it tends to only flow the join. If you use your flame on the entire

Jump rings cut from 14-gauge fine silver wire.

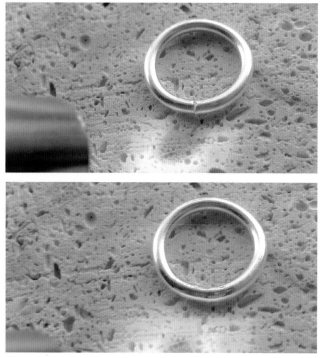

For an easy fuse, simply heat the kiln brick in front of the join. This is easy to do correctly as you can just "light up" the brick, by making it red-hot. The ring will evenly heat and fuse on its own, only at the join.

TIP	CLOSING JUMP RINGS

The easiest way to close a jump ring is to bring it slightly past the join in either direction, creating spring tension, then close it.

surface of the ring, you risk flowing the whole surface of the ring. You may or may not want to do this; it really depends on the look you're going for in your finished piece. A fully flowed piece will have a rougher and more porous surface, which might be to your advantage if you're creating metalwork meant to appear antique or to take on a rich patina.

5 Once the metal at the joint flows, immediately remove the flame. If you hold the flame on the work even a second too long, the joint, which is the hottest part, will flow apart and be ruined. Learn to rotate your torch flame up and down on the kiln brick without changing your basic hand position. This will give you great control over your flame.

6 Use protective tweezers to pick up the ring and quench it and the tweezer tips in the water-filled bowl.

7 Use the hammer and anvil to texture the ring as desired.

8 Repeat Steps 3 to 7 to make as many closed rings as will fill half the desired chain length.
   Both your torch tip and kiln brick will get very hot as you work, so take care not to burn yourself on them, and train yourself to touch the water in your quench bowl before you pick up the quenched rings. If the water feels warm, do not touch the ring or quenched item. Change the water in the quench bowl without touching the potentially still-hot metal piece in the water.

9 Use 1 open jump ring to connect 2 fused rings, making sure your joint is clean and tight. Place the two already-fused rings vertically in a small channel dug in your kiln brick. The channel should be deep enough to support the rings, but not so deep that the ring you're fusing touches the finished rings standing on end.

10 Fuse the new ring as if it were the only ring on your brick. Since it's not touching the other two rings, there's no danger that they will fuse together, even if you flow

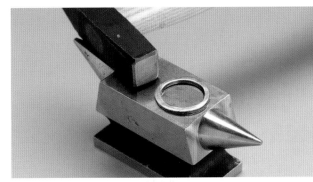

I use the chasing side of my riveting hammer for forging, hardening, and most general-purpose hammering.

Plain rings look beautiful with light forging.

the entire surface of the new ring. Use tweezers to pick up the length of chain and quench. You can forge the new ring or leave as is; it's a lovely look to alternate heavily forged and plain round links in a handmade chain.

11 Connect the chain's end link to another fused ring with a newly added ring. Make sure your new join is clean and tight. Stand the two rings it adjoins on end in the channel, piling the extra ring or rings on the brick behind it. Fuse the new ring as before. Quench the entire chain and tweezer's tips. Repeat to fuse all the rings together into a chain of your desired length.

12 Once the chain is complete, work-harden the links by hammering them one at a time on an anvil. Be careful not to mar the neighboring links as you hammer. Work-harden a bit of the link, turn it, do some more, turn it again. You may also tumble your chain for a lovely surface polish, but only hammering or forging will fully work-harden the chain.

The kiln brick makes fused chain easy; just dig a small channel to support the two closed rings on either side of your active ring. Pile up extra links on the brick as your chain grows.

Remember to work-harden each link on a block or anvil, turning the ring so that all parts of it are hammered.

RESOURCES

METAL CLAY, METAL TOOLS, AND FINDINGS FOR METALSMITHING

Rio Grande
(800) 545-6566
7500 Bluewater Dr.
Albuquerque, NM 87121-1962
riogrande.com

Cool Tools
(888) 478-5060
cooltools.us

Whaley Studios
Jay Whaley
(619) 299-9619
3848 5th Ave.
San Diego, CA 92103
whaleystudios.com

Metal Clay Findings
(888) 999-6404
49 Hurdis St.
North Providence, RI 02904-4905
metalclayfindings.com

FELT BALLS, DISCS, AND FLOWER SHAPES

Handbehg.com
St. Louis, MO
handbehg.com

PRESSED BRASS FLOWERS AND LEAF SHAPES, UNUSUAL SEQUINS, RESIN FLOWERS, HANDMADE FELT COMPONENTS, AND UNUSUAL FINDINGS

Gail Crosman Moore
71 Creamery Hill Rd.
W. Orange, MA 01364
gailcrosmanmoore.com

Objects & Elements
objectsandelements.com

Eclectica
(262) 641-0910
18900 W. Bluemound Rd.
Brookfield, WI 53045
eclecticabeads.com

BEADING WIRE, CRIMPS, AND OTHER BEADY TOOLS AND SUPPLIES

Soft Flex Company
(866) 925-FLEX
softflexcompany.com

Fusion Beads
(888) 781-3559
13024 Stone Ave. N
Seattle, WA 98133
fusionbeads.com

SEED BEADS AND SEED-BEADY SUPPLIES

Beyond Beadery
(800) 840-5548
PO Box 460
Rollinsville, CO 80474-0460
beyondbeadery.com

Fire Mountain Gems and Beads
(source of the Nymo on the 3 oz spools)
(800) 423-2319
firemountaingems.com

Jane's Fiber and Beads
(423) 639-7919
janesfiberandbeads.com

The Red Bead
(707) 253-2323
3209 Jefferson St.
Napa, CA 94558
theredbead.com

Note: The Delica bead colors used in Peep Cuff, page 44, are DB1010 and DB1012.

BEADMAKERS

Sarah Moran
Z-Beads
z-beads.com

Bronwen Heilman
Tucson, AZ
bronwenheilman.com

Joyce Rooks
San Diego, CA
joycerooks.com

Isis Ray
Carnation, WA
isisray.com

Libby Leuchtmann
Third Degree Glass Factory
5200 Delmar Blvd.
St. Louis, MO 63108-1028
thirddegreeglassfactory.com

RAM'S HORN, BALL-END, AND ONE-OF-A-KIND CLASPS AND KITS

Kate McKinnon Designs
Tucson, AZ
katemckinnon.com

HANDMADE WIREWORKED CLASPS AND KITS

Barb Switzer
(707) 722-1955
PO Box 257
Redcrest, CA 95569-0257
beadswitzer.com

GALLERY ARTISTS

Grant Diffendaffer
diffendaffer.com

Karen Flowers
kflow3@yahoo.com

Tom Holland
(870) 363-4890

Amy Johnson and Cynthia Archer
Tank Studio and Proper Jewelry
Toronto
tankstudio.ca

Gail Crosman Moore
gailcrosmanmoore.com

Sarah Moran
Z-Beads
z-beads.com

Kelly Russell
25 Mansion Rd.
Linthicum, MD 21090

Teresa Sullivan
teresasullivanstudio.com

Cynthia Toops and Dan Adams
cdbeads.biz

Kate Valleroy
The Red Anvil
St. Louis, MO
redanvilart.com

Kim Van Antwerp
cuteglassbeads.com

ABOUT THE AUTHOR

Kate McKinnon is a mixed-media artist who lives and works in Tucson, Arizona. Her work focuses on the engineering of how elements work together, connect, and grow into finished pieces of jewelry. She has made a life study of small tasks, always asking, "How could this be better, stronger, simpler, or more elegant?"

Kate has been beading since she was a child and working with metal and metal clay since 1998. She won the prestigious Rio Grande Saul Bell award in 2005 for her innovative design with metal clay. Kate travels the world to teach and speak about jewelry design. She is the author of four books, including *Sculptural Metal Clay Jewelry* (Interweave, 2010).

INDEX

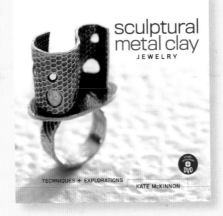
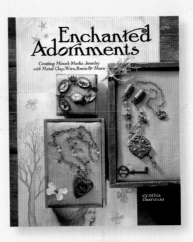